Photo Keepsakes

by *Suzanne McNeill*

Leisure Arts, Inc.
and
Oxmoor House, Inc.

Dedicated to my daughter,
Lani Stiles.
Every year our family takes
hundreds of photos. Lani and I
have spent countless hours
organizing them into
Scrapbooks, keepsakes,
and our Family Memories.

Credits

Art Directors - Janet Long, Laurie Rice • Cover Design - Trey Sprinkle
Managing Director - Kathy McMillan • Artists - Patty Williams & Marti Wyble
Keepsakes Editor - Lani Stiles • Keepsakes Crafts - Delores Frantz & Cyndi Hansen
Photographers - Donna & David Thomason
Instructions Editors - Wanda J. Little & Colleen Reigh

Printed in the United States of America
First Printing

Library of Congress
Catalog Card
Number 98-065091

Hardcover
ISBN 1-57486-091-7

Softcover
ISBN 1-57486-108-5

Leisure Arts, Inc.
P.O. Box 55595
Little Rock, AR 72215

The best keepsakes
are personalized with photos.
Special gifts will be
treasured forever.

Table of Contents

While I was growing up, my father smoked cigars. I saved many of the cigar boxes to hold pencils and other treasures. One box that endured through the years protected a collection of childhood photographs. The pictures became a constant source of interest for my daughter, Lani. She was fascinated with the people that made up her family history.

Asking who all the people in the pictures represented, Lani raised a few questions I didn't know the answers to. My mother, called Nanny by her grandchildren, is the archive of information. The antique photographs are a mystery without her. How ironic to treasure the photographs without knowing who is in them.

A chest for safe keeping was the first home of my keepsakes. The photographs, the antique camera, a dried flower and my Grandmother Bea Bea's wedding ring filled the treasure trunk. When the box began to overflow, a long overdue effort to care for the valuable photographic mementos of my family history was set into motion.

First, a search and rescue mission allowed me to rediscover all the treasures. Second, restorative research introduced me to new ways to protect the items from the deteriorating effects of bright light, humidity and dust. By simply framing, encasing or duplicating the photos and keepsakes, I saved them from further deterioration.

I not only wanted to preserve the items but also to display them in my home and places where I could enjoy them. Hanging on a prominent wall, the tokens became a permanent reminder of my family's traditions and remembrances of the most treasured moments in life.

Suzanne

$\mathscr{I}$ adore photographs and all the memories they conjure! The instant I lay eyes on the image of family, friends or places, my heart swells with the excitement of remembering a special time from days past.

While growing up, I collected photographs of family and friends, not to mention a good many keepsakes handed down for generations. I took them with me to my first home which was small and didn't even have an attic or basement for storage. Surrounded by boxes of my favorite things, I began to hang the photographs, keepsakes and memorabilia in the rooms where I lived. Though I have since moved and my children have grown, I still love to be encircled by my treasures. The pictures have not changed but the frames have.

In this book, I hope to share with you wonderful ideas for using photographs, keepsakes and collections to enliven the rooms of your home, to adorn the materials you wear and to surround yourself with heartwarming images. The following pages offer a wealth of inspiration for new ways to use photographs to embellish throw pillows, a Victorian vest, a memory frame for the hallway, holiday ornaments and much more!

Suzanne

Vintage Photos

The enduring appeal of vintage keepsakes are classic reminders of the significance of historical value even when the items themselves may have little monetary worth. A few photographs and keepsakes can easily be turned into the most precious of possessions when they represent the life and times of family generations.

My Grandmother Bea Bea took a special interest in serving the best of meals in her home. To serve the decadent desserts, she employed a polished silver spoon with a handle of carved ivory. Among the things passed down to me, was Bea Bea's spoon collection. I took pride in the gift and its history. Along with mounted photographs of my grandmother and her sisters, a spoon shelf now holds the family's collection of antiques.

Suzanne

*T*race your family tree to discover your roots. A family album has long been a protective place for special photographs and memories. Dress up the best of the photos with delicate lace.

Lace Your Family History

by Debi Linker

MATERIALS: Two 9" x 12" pieces of heavy matboard, Two ¾" x 11¾" pieces of heavy matboard, Two 8¾" x 11" pieces of lightweight matboard, 5" x 7" precut matboard photo frame, Two pieces of 10" x 12" and One piece of 5" x 7" thin batting, ½ yard of Cream moiré fabric, ⅜ yard of coordinating lining fabric, ⅓ yard of 6" bridal lace, 1½ yards ⅝" wired ribbon, Narrow lace to fit inside opening of frame, 2 yards each of 2 colors of 4mm silk ribbon, *Creative Beginnings* Creative Corners CK101 and CK103 (24K gold plate) or CK201 and CK203 (sterling silver plate), 1½ yards of *HeatnBond*, Hot glue, GOOP glue

Instructions on page 14

For elegant pages, mount your precious wedding photos and mementos with ribbons, lacy doilies and Victorian cutouts. Gold corners add the finishing touch.

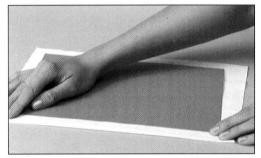

1 Apply batting to the front and back covers, then cover matboard with fabric, fusing edges to the back.

2 Hot glue lace and trims on the front of the cover.

3 Embellish the photo mat and glue it on the cover.

4 Glue gold corners in place as shown.

TO MAKE COVERS

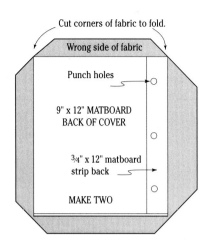

Cut corners of fabric to fold.

Wrong side of fabric

Punch holes

9" x 12" MATBOARD
BACK OF COVER

¾" x 12" matboard
strip back

MAKE TWO

Turn fabric under at corners and fuse.

MATBOARD
BACK OF COVER

Cut corners of
fabric to fold
over matboard.

Wrong side of fabric

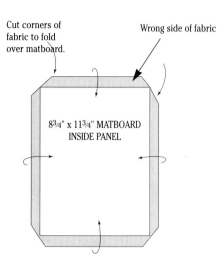

8¾" x 11¾" MATBOARD
INSIDE PANEL

Fuse inside panel to cover.

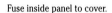

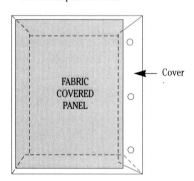

FABRIC
COVERED
PANEL

Cover

Lace Your Family History

INSTRUCTIONS:

Cover - Use a sheet of notebook paper for alignment and punch 3 holes in ¾" matboard strips. Place two sets of 9" x 12" and ¾" x 11¾" pieces side by side and cover each set as one piece. Apply batting to the front and back covers. Cut two pieces of fabric 11¾" x 13½". Apply *HeatnBond* to back of fabric following the manufacturer's instructions. Place fabric on the matboards with seam allowance overlapping evenly on all sides. Fuse fabric to matboards. Fuse seam allowances to back of boards.

Lace - Glue lace across top of cover and glue raw edges to back.

Lining - Cover two lightweight matboards with lining fabric following the cover instructions. Position covered boards on the back of cover and hot glue in place.

Frame - Cover the top of the matboard photo frame with batting and then with fabric. Cover only the top of frame. Pull wire on one edge of wired ribbon and gather to fit outside of the frame. Hot glue the pulled edge to back of frame. Use GOOP to glue small gold corners to edges of photo cutout as shown in photo. Carefully hot glue narrow lace to the edge of frame opening. Position the frame on one cover and hot glue two sides and the bottom edge to the album. Leave top edge open to insert photo.

Finish - Use GOOP to glue large gold corners to the album. Use an ice pick to make holes through fabric over holes in narrow matboard strips. Insert photo album pages. Use a needle to pull silk ribbon through holes in front, album pages and back. Start in center hole on back of album, then lace through the bottom hole, across back to top hole and back to center. Tie ends in a bow.

Photo Frame

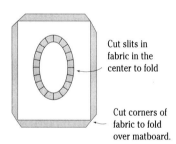

Cut slits in
fabric in the
center to fold

Cut corners of
fabric to fold
over matboard.

TIE COVERS

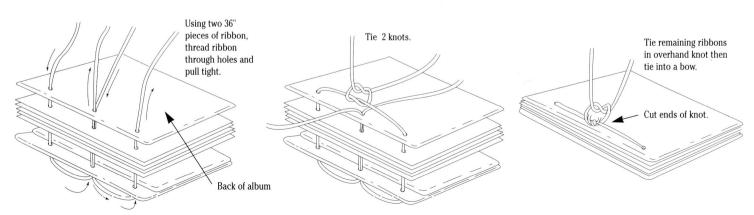

Using two 36"
pieces of ribbon,
thread ribbon
through holes and
pull tight.

Back of album

Tie 2 knots.

Tie remaining ribbons
in overhand knot then
tie into a bow.

Cut ends of knot.

*M*ary *Poppins says, "A spoonful of sugar helps the medicine go down." Keep your fancy serving spoons in a shelf for pretty display. Grandma did and it gave her a place to show the collection to all her friends. Include antique photographs, too, in this one of a kind spoon shelf.*

Spoon Full of Honey

by Jean Mollard

MATERIALS: *Artifacts* Metal Carvings (three 15412 oval frames, four 16262 large corners, two 15332 leaf corners), 3 Pale Green 236 tassels, Walnut Hollow broom holder shelf, 3 yards of Pale Green gimp tape, 3 photos, Felt square, Rose and Pale Green acrylic paint, Antiquing liquid, GOOP glue, Hot glue, Silver and Gold paint pens

INSTRUCTIONS: Paint shelf Rose, let dry. Dab with Pale Green paint, apply antiquing liquid while still wet to blend colors. Paint metal pieces Silver and highlight with Gold. Cut photos and felt to fit frames, glue in place. Glue gimp around shelf edges using hot glue. Glue frames and corners to shelf using GOOP. Hang tassels and spoons on shelf.

1 Paint shelf Pink, dab with Pale Green then apply antiquing

2 Paint metal pieces Silver, highlight with Gold.

3 Glue photos in frames with GOOP glue.

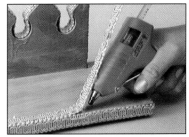

4 Hot glue gimp tape around edges of the shelf.

Photos-In-A-Box

by Melissa Helbig

MATERIALS: *CorDecor* Create-a-Heart jewelry box, Gold cherub gift wrap, 2 yards of ⅝" Black/Gold ribbon, 1 yard of ¾" Greek key ribbon, 1 yard of 2" Black fringe, Three 1" gold heart charms, Gold foiled paper, Gold foiled bird stickers, Gold and Black acrylic paint, Small sponge, Decorative edge scissors, White glue, Hot glue, Photos

INSTRUCTIONS:

Box - Cover outside of box with paper. Cover both sides of drawers and top and bottom box pieces with paper. Paint uncovered pieces Gold. Sponge drawer pieces with Black. Assemble box following the manufacturer's instructions.

Drawer Pulls - Cut three 1" pieces of ⅝" ribbon, fold in thirds and sew a heart charm in the center. Glue a pull to the center front of each drawer.

Photos - Copy photos on a copy machine. Trim photo copies with decorative scissors. Glue on box with foiled paper backgrounds and frames.

Trim - Glue ⅝" ribbon along hinges and inside box seams. Glue ¾" ribbon around outside bottom of box and fringe around top of box. Use remaining ⅝" ribbon for ties.

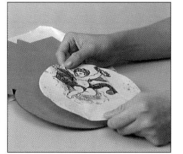

1 Cover the box pieces with paper.

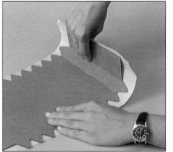

2 Fold pieces and assemble box.

3 Trim and glue photo copies in place.

4 Glue on ribbons and braid trim.

by Mary Jo Hiney

Decorate your photos with elegant fabric and ribbons to bring back memories of days past. Fabrics and ribbons add elegance to any room.

Tie a Pink Ribbon Around the Old Family Tree

MATERIALS:
24" of ¾" Gold metallic lace, 3" Pink tassel, Ribbons (12" of 1½" Pink satin, 24" of ¹⁄₁₆" Pink satin, 1¼ yards of 1" Pink ombre wired, 15" of 13mm Rose, 15" of 7mm Pink), *Creative Beginnings* 1108 gold 'Mother' charm, Two 2½" gold frames

INSTRUCTIONS:

Book mark - Weave ¹⁄₁₆" ribbon through lace. Overlap lace ⅛" on 1½" ribbon and stitch in place, iron flat. Fold ribbon in half lengthwise with right sides together and stitch a diagonal seam at one end. Trim seam, turn right side out and iron flat.

Rose - Make a gathered rose with ombre ribbon. Shape rose.

Small Rose - Place 7mm ribbon on 13mm ribbon matching edges. Make a gathered rose.

Finish - Glue large rose to top and tassel to bottom of bookmark. Glue small rose on top of tassel.

Photo Screen and Gathered Rose instructions on page 18. Oval Hat Pin instructions on page 19.

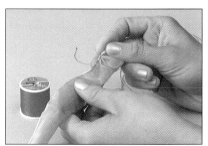

1 Fold end of ribbon at a 45° angle, fold again and roll 3 times. Secure folds, gather edge.

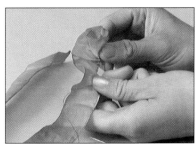

2 Gather long edge with a needle and thread. Pull tight, wrap around center and secure.

3 Assemble hanger. Glue photo frames and charm in place.

Cut 2 Fabric
Cut 2 Cardboard
Add ¾" to all edges of fabric

CENTER OF SCREEN

Photo Screen

by Mary Jo Hiney

PAGE 16 PHOTO

MATERIALS: *Creative Beginnings* Memory Embellishments: Eight CK101 corners (2 pkgs.), Four CK103 corners (1 pkg.), One each brass charms 2213 shoe, 1250 open heart, 18" x 24" piece of matboard, ⅜ yard of 45" Dark Blue fabric, ⅓ yard of batting, 1⅝ yards of ¼" Gold cord, Two 1" x 9" strips of HeatnBond, Hot glue, 4 photos

INSTRUCTIONS FOR SCREEN:

Screen - Trace screen patterns. Cut 2 center sections, 2 left and 2 right sections from matboard. Cut Dark Blue fabric ¾" larger than patterns. Cut 2 strips of fabric 1¼" x 19". Pad each matboard section with batting and wrap with fabric.

Hinges - Fuse HeatnBond to narrow strips of fabric. Fold in half, fuse for 9" finished length. Leaving ½" of hinge between sections, Glue hinges to back center and side sections with Hot glue as shown.

Assembly - Glue front sections to back sections. Glue cord around screen beginning on center bottom of one side using Hot glue. Glue photos, corners and heart on screen.

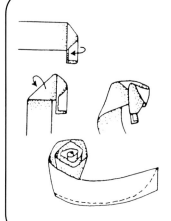

ROSETTE. Fold ribbon at a 45° angle with ½" tail. Fold again. Fold edge of ribbon diagonally back and wrap around center. Secure each wrap with thread. Continue to wrap and roll for ½ of ribbon. Gather bottom edge of remaining ribbon tapering thread at end. Pull up gathers, wrap around rose, secure.

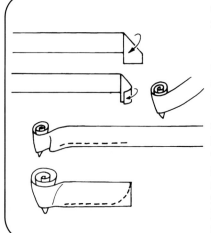

GATHERED ROSE. Fold ribbon at a 45° angle with ½" tail. Roll ribbon 3 times and secure with thread. Take a ⅛" tuck and secure. Roll ribbon slightly and take another ⅛" tuck, secure. Measure half of remaining ribbon and gather. Pull tight, wrap around center and secure. Gather remaining ribbon curving stitches to opposite side at end. Pull tight, wrap and secure.

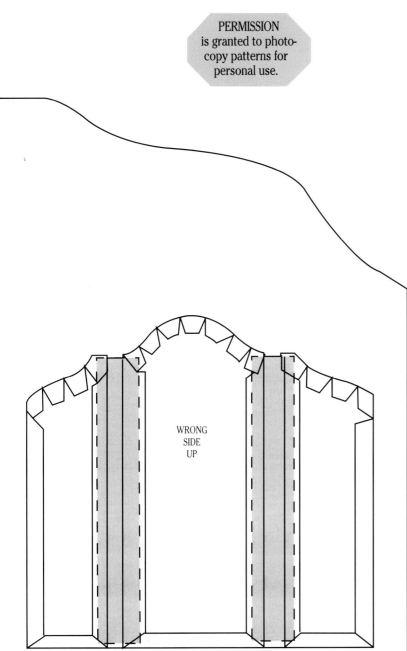

WRONG
SIDE
UP

½" SPACE   HINGE

SIDES OF SCREEN

Cut 2 Fabric on right side
Cut 4 Cardboard
Cut 2 Fabric on wrong side
Add ¾" to all edges of fabric

Oval Hat Pin

by Mary Jo Hiney

PAGE 16 PHOTO

MATERIALS: *Creative Beginnings* Brass Charms: 2676 hat pin blank, 99559 jumprings, 6235 oval setting, 4824 oval frame, 1457 heart, 4mm silk ribbon (Rose, Burgundy, Old Rose, Navy, Khaki, Beige), 2" x 4" piece of Rose fabric, 2" square of batting, 2" x 4" piece of cardboard, five 5mm Black rhinestones

INSTRUCTIONS:

Ovals - Cut 2 large ovals and one small oval from cardboard using patterns. Cut 2 pieces of fabric for large ovals. Cut one piece of fabric for small oval. Wrap large ovals with fabric. Pad and wrap small oval. Glue top of hat pin blank to back of one large wrapped oval. Let dry. Glue this piece to back of large brass oval with loop on brass piece facing down. Glue second wrapped large oval to front of larger brass piece directly over opening. Cut the loop off the smaller brass piece. Place small wrapped oval in center of small brass oval. Fold the tabs down to secure the cardboard. Glue on the larger piece of brass covering the cardboard oval already in place.

Rosettes - Make 8 rosettes and 7 rosebuds using 5" of 4mm ribbon each. Glue rosettes and 4 rosebuds on center oval. Glue rhinestones randomly around rosettes.

Finish - Attach brass heart to loop at bottom of larger brass oval using a jumpring. Glue 3 rosebuds to center of heart. Insert pin in the screen.

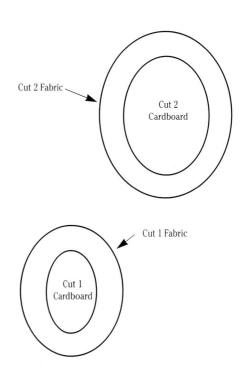

Cut 2 Fabric

Cut 2
Cardboard

Cut 1 Fabric

Cut 1
Cardboard

1 Collect your favorite photos and charms that reflect the personality of the loved one.

2 Trim photos and insert in frames.

3 Use the jumprings to attach the frames and charms to the necklace.

She's the one who always sent a card on your birthday. She's the one who always baked you pies and cookies. This ornamental necklace is a special piece designed just for remembering her.

Grandmother Remembers

by Debi Linker

MATERIALS: *Creative Beginnings* WAM90001 necklace and frame set, Two WAM90002 frames, One WAM90011 sewing set, WAM90009 boy and girl charms (24K Gold Plate), or WAM90016, 90017, 90026, and 90024 (Sterling Silver Plate), Needle nose pliers

INSTRUCTIONS: Cut photos to fit frame backs. Layer the photo over the cardboard spacers and under the clear plastic. Insert the set into the frame. Attach the charms and frames to the necklace with the jumprings included in each package. Use one jumpring per charm or frame. Slip the needle nose pliers into the jumpring and gently spread the ends enough to insert them through the loop of the charm and the chain. Exert gentle pressure on the ring to bring the ends together for closing. The jumprings can attach to specific links on the chain or can be attached around the chain to allow the charms and frames to slide.

A photo of an adored, favorite aunt. An heirloom pair of earrings that were Grandma's. An antique cameo broach. These simple elements that so enrich a family's history are celebrated here in a memorable way. A collection of brass charm pins adorned with family photos will become treasured family heirlooms.

A Charmed Existence
by Pam Hammons

Safari
MATERIALS: *Creative Beginnings* (2965 lion, 2962 elephant, 2963 giraffe, 2967 zebra, 4604 round blank, 2638 pin back), Photo

Mother
MATERIALS: *Creative Beginnings* (1109 'Mother', 2638 pin back, 1250 heart frame), Photo

Locket
MATERIALS: *Creative Beginnings* (4402 cherub, 1825 locket, 2638 pin back), 2 photos

Shoe/Doily
MATERIALS: *Creative Beginnings* (2213 shoe, 4604 round blank, 2638 pin back), 4" crocheted doily, Photo

Oval
MATERIALS: *Creative Beginnings* (2203 rose open oval, 5001 oval blank, 2638 pin back), Photo

1 Select brass pieces, photos and embellishments.

2 Trim photos to fit brass blanks.

3 Assemble the pins using GOOP or E6000 glue.

A wedding reception table is graced with an elegant silver and white photo candle.

A graduation party to celebrate one of life's biggest accomplishments is magnified by the light of a large pillar candle.

Light up any occasion with your own celebration candle.

The Light of the Party
by Genevieve Neglia

Wedding Candle
MATERIALS: 9" White pillar candle, *Distlefink* (1 sheet of White Wax Impressions Sheet Wax 56001, 2 strips of Silver Braid Wax Lace Wrap 56305, Sheet of Silver Foiled Cherub CandleStickers 54606, 1 package of Candle Magic Stick-Ums 51740), 5" of White strung pearls, White satin ribbon, 3 White ribbon roses, Bell, Floral spray, Wedding photo

INSTRUCTIONS: Place wax sheet face down, trim to fit candle. Apply Stick-Ums to back edges of wrap and press firmly around candle. Use Stick-Ums to apply Silver braid at top and bottom of candle and attach photo. Peel and press stickers in place. Add embellishments.

Graduation Candle
MATERIALS: 9" White pillar candle, *Distlefink* (1 sheet of Gold Starburst CandleStickers 54301, 1 package of Candle Magic Stick-Ums 51740, 1 sheet of Gold Foiled Honeycomb 55401), Red/Gold tassel, Graduation card, Star shaped cookie cutter

INSTRUCTIONS: Trim card and photo. Cut out stars. Apply with Stick-Ums. Attach candle stickers and tie a tassel around the candle.

Birthday Candle
MATERIALS: White square candle, *Distlefink* (1 sheet of Balloon CandleStickers 54502, 1 package of Candle Magic Stick-Ums 51740), Assorted ribbons, Photo, 2 small balloons

INSTRUCTIONS: Peel and press stickers on candle. Trim photo and attach with Stick-Ums. Add ribbons and balloons.

1 Collect supplies to embellish a candle.

2 Trim wax sheet to fit candle, wrap around candle.

3 Peel and press stickers on candle.

A collage of bits and pieces makes the perfect frame-up. Choose a theme, arrange the pieces and you will double the significance of a specially framed photo.

Frame-Up

by Pam Hammons

Wedding

MATERIALS: Shadow box frame with mat, Decorative scissors, Printed caption, Photo, Wedding boutonniere and headpiece

INSTRUCTIONS: Trim the caption paper using decorative scissors. Arrange and glue items in place.

Baby

MATERIALS: Baby photos and mementos, 11" x 14" Shadow box frame, Lace and ribbon to fit around edge of background, Gold marker, Decorative edge scissors, Piece of heavy paper

INSTRUCTIONS: Remove frame insert. Thread ribbon through edge of lace and glue lace on insert mitering the corners. Trim photos and caption paper with decorative scissors. Write name and birth date with a marker. Arrange and glue items in place. Replace insert and secure.

1 Collect photos, mementos, lace and ribbon.

2 Remove frame insert. Arrange and glue items in place.

3 Replace insert in frame and secure.

Coasters with Class
by Pam Hammons

MATERIALS: *Ehlers Company* Gold foiled paper die cuts, *M.C.G. Textiles* acrylic coasters, Colored cardstock, Photos, Gold marker

INSTRUCTIONS: Cut cardstock to fit inside the coaster. Trim the photos and frame with gold die cuts. Add captions with a Gold marker.

1 Trim the gold die cuts into circles or ovals to frame photos.

2 Insert decorated paper in coaster and replace cork backing.

Crystal Memories Candleholder
by Delores Frantz

MATERIALS: *Sweet Gallery* Shades of Light candleholder, *Charmingly Yours* (1819 oval frame, 1328 bow charm), Pale Green gimp tape, Photo, Goop glue

INSTRUCTIONS: Glue gimp around top and bottom of shade. Trim photo to fit oval frame. Glue photo, frame and bow in place.

Bend the frame to fit curve of shade. Glue braid, charm and frame on shade.

*R*each for those treasured keepsakes you've been storing on the top shelf. Add a touch of photo personality to ordinary objects like a glass jar, a special fabric bag or an old book. These keepsakes make great gifts.

A Winning Combination
by Linda Lamberton

Bottle

Collect the embellishments and photos.
MATERIALS: *Sweet Gallery* (Heart bottle, Pansy cork stopper, Brass accents), Photo, Ribbon roses, Buttons, Beads, Assorted embellishments, GOOP glue

Glue embellishments on bottle using GOOP.

Bag

MATERIALS: Fabric bag with tassel trim, 3" crocheted doily, 6" of 2" lace, 3" tatted doily, Assorted buttons, 4" of strung pearls, Spanish moss, *Creative Beginnings* Mother charm, Photo

Glue embellishments in top of bag using GOOP.

Book

MATERIALS: *Wimpole Street* Battenburg lace motif, Small old book, ¼" satin ribbon, Assorted buttons, *Creative Beginnings* Hand charm, 3" tassel, ¼" braid, Feather, 3 ribbon roses, Photo
INSTRUCTIONS: Open book to center pages. Arrange and glue embellishments on book referring to photo for placement.

*R*emember those oatmeal chocolate chip cookies steaming with a mouth watering smell when you were growing up? Continue the cookie tradition by serving a tray full of delicious homemade memories.

Serving Up Memories

by Judi Kauffman

MATERIALS: *Sudberry House* trays, Assorted photos, Mementos or Collections, Small pieces of trim, White glue

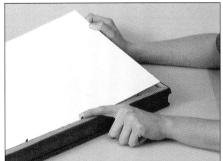

1 Remove backing, insert and glass from tray.

2 Arrange and glue photos and embellishments on insert.

3 Clean glass. Reassemble the tray.

*I*mmigrants landed at Ellis Island with all their worldly belongings packed in trunks. Even after settling in new homes, valuables were often stored in trunks for safe keeping. Make your own trunk to preserve the special objects that express your heritage.

For Safe Keeping

by Cyndi Hansen

MATERIALS: Old cosmetic case, *Artifacts* vintage paper, Spray primer, Decoupage glue, Gold acrylic paint, Paintbrush, fabric, 6" x 10½" piece of cardboard, ½" Gold ribbon, yards of Gold gimp tape, Seven ⅝" buttons, Quilt batting, Craft knife, Small screwdriver, Spray sealer, Hot glue

INSTRUCTIONS:

Case - Clean case and remove any straps from inside the case. Spray primer on the case. Paint hardware and trim Gold.

Paper - With the lid closed and beginning at the top of case, cut a piece of paper slightly larger than each area to be covered. Center paper piece over each area and use your fingernail to crease the paper next to trim. (If necessary, clip excess paper to allow paper to lie flat.) To work around handle, mark a dot on paper for center of each handle end. Use a craft knife to cut a small X in paper at each mark. Make a straight cut from the closest edge of paper to each X. Make small cuts in paper around hardware until paper can wrap snugly around it. Working on one area at a time, spray adhesive on back of paper, press paper on case and use your fingers to smooth out bubbles and wrinkles. Trim paper as needed. Continue until case is covered. To seal case, apply a spray sealer.

Lining - To determine the length of fabric piece for inside bottom of case, measure inside of case from top of left side down across bottom and up right side, add 2 ". For width of fabric piece, measure from front of case down across bottom and up back side, add 2". Cut fabric piece. Place fabric piece in bottom of case bringing excess up over sides. Beginning at one side, use screwdriver to gently tuck fabric between case and lining. For corners, trim fabric and tuck edges under, glue. Repeat for lid, glueing fabric to back of lid.

Lid Liner - Line top of case. Cut a piece of cardboard to fit inside the lid. Glue batting on cardboard. Cut a piece of fabric 2" larger on all sides than cardboard, wrap fabric around cardboard and glue edges on back. Glue ribbon and buttons as shown. Glue in lid to hold photos and cards.

Trim - Glue gimp over edges of fabric on top and bottom of case.

1 Spray case with primer and paint Gold.

2 Trim paper and glue to each section of case.

3 Line case with fabric. Pad and cover cardboard for lid liner.

4 Glue padded liner inside top of case.

Crazy quilts traditionally combine a collection of fabric scraps from old clothes, but today handsome pillows, vests and crazy quilts showcase exquisite fabrics like silk, satin, brocade, tapestry and lace. If you wear a few photos on a vest, you're sure to receive inquiries about those you display so close to your heart.

A Vested Interest

by Cyndi Hansen and Virginia Reynolds

MATERIALS: *Hues Photo Effects* transfer paper, 16 Photos, Purchased pattern for vest, Muslin, Black lining fabric, ¼ yard of Cream satin fabric for photos, Assorted fabric scraps, 2 yards each of 4 assorted lace trims, 4 yards of lace trim for edging on vest, Ribbon, Washable fabric glue, Light-weight paper-backed fusible web, Deckle edge scissors

INSTRUCTIONS:

Crazy Quilt - Using vest pattern, cut front and back from muslin. Cut front and back lining pieces from Black. Use a color copy machine to copy photos onto *Photo Effects* transfer paper. Trim photos on transfer paper with deckle scissors then use an iron to transfer photos to Cream fabric spacing photos 4" apart. Note: Cover transfer with muslin before ironing. Following manufacturer's instructions, fuse web to wrong side of transfers and fabric scraps. Using photo as a guide, trim edges of transfer fabric, remove paper backing and place on muslin vest pieces, fuse in place with an iron. Cut different shapes and sizes from scrap fabrics to fit around transfers cutting shapes slightly larger than needed to allow for overlap. Remove paper backing from shapes and fuse in place overlapping edges slightly. Sew or glue lace over raw edges of fabrics. **Vest** - Following pattern instructions, make vest. Pin lace trim around outside edge of vest and sew in place.

1 Transfer photo to fabric.

2 Fuse photo to muslin (cover the photo).

3 Arrange crazy quilt pieces.

4 Fabric glue trim in place.

traveler always starts an adventure with a journal to keep notes by day and write down thoughts by night. Leather bound covers protect the crisp white, blank pages. Even the look of leather brings to mind adventures in far away places.

Leather or Not?
by Kari Lee

MATERIALS: *The Leather Factory* (Two 8½" x 11" leather trim pieces, 24" of ⅛" Natural leather lace, 3/16" drive punch and mallet, Leather Sheen, Leathercraft cement), Matboard (4" x 8¼" for front support, 5¼" x 8¼" for back support, 4" x 4" for easel support), 25 sheets of 8¼" x 5¼" heavy weight paper, Rubber brayer, Water base markers (Red, Yellow, Brown), White paint pen, Embossing heat tool, Bone burnisher, Bristle brush, Metal ruler, *All Night Media* rubber stamps (543F Compass Rose, 327E Around the World, 333E On the Road, 308E Suitcase, 554E Wish Postmark), *Tsukineko, Inc.* Fabrico stamp pads (Ultramarine, Real Black, Cool Gray, Chocolate), Craft knife, Old map, Cutting mat, White photo corners, Photos

INSTRUCTIONS:

Leather - Cut two pieces 5½" x 8½" for front and back, two easel pieces referring to diagram and one piece 2½" x 8½" for gusset. Cut a 2½" x 4" opening in center of front piece 1" from bottom. Cut a 2½" x ⅛" slit in center of back piece 4" from bottom. Stamp frame front as shown. Use brayer to apply Ultramarine ink directly on remaining leather frame parts. Lightly heat set inks on all leather parts with embossing heat tool. Hold heat tool at least 6" away from leather and move tool continuously or the leather will scorch. Add color to stamped images and edges of Ultramarine leather parts with markers. Let dry. Spray two light coats of Leather Sheen on all leather pieces to seal. Do not omit this step.

Support - Cut map to cover matboard supports leaving ¾" on each side to fold under. Apply leather cement to one side of each matboard, center on map pieces. Press to secure. Fold edges to back and glue.

Easel - Cut matboard referring to diagram. Apply leather cement to matboard, center on back of one leather piece and glue remaining leather piece in place.

Pages - Mark and punch 4 holes in heavy paper 1⅛" from side edge, ½" from top and 2" apart.

Frame - Cement gusset piece on top edge of leather front and back overlapping ¾". Let dry. Burnish both folds on top of leather easel arm open. Insert the flaps into slit of frame backing from the colored side of leather. Apply cement and press to secure. Let dry. Coat entire back of back support matboard with cement. Position mat support ⅛" from bottom edge and sides of inside back cover of frame. Press to secure. Let dry. On front matboard support, apply cement to sides and bottom edge. Position mat support on front inside flap of frame. Once frame has been completed photo can be inserted through unglued top edge of board. On assembled frame, use a piece of the punched paper and a pencil to mark position of holes. Working on a solid surface use drive punch and mallet to punch holes through layers of leather and matboard. Twist punch carefully when removing from hole. Color top side of lace with Red marker. Seal with Leather Sheen. Let dry. Cut lace in half. Thread lace ends evenly through 2 holes from back of frame, through paper and out front of frame. Secure lace ends on the front of frame with an overhand knot. Repeat for other holes.

Pages - Mount photos on pages with photo corners.

1 Cut leather pieces using a craft knife, metal ruler and mat.

2 Rubber stamp front leather piece.

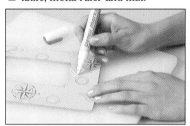
3 Color stamp images with detail markers.

4 Punch holes and tie album together with lace.

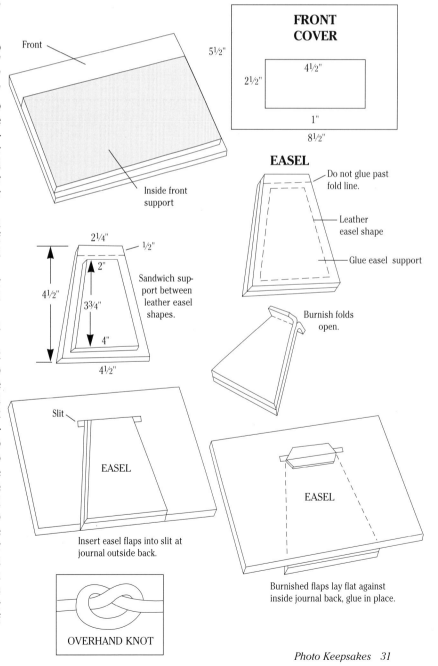

FRONT COVER
4½"
2½"
1"
8½"
5½"

Front
Inside front support

EASEL
Do not glue past fold line.
Leather easel shape
Glue easel support
Burnish folds open.

2¼"
½"
2"
3¾"
4"
4½"
4½"

Sandwich support between leather easel shapes.

Slit
EASEL
Insert easel flaps into slit at journal outside back.

EASEL
Burnished flaps lay flat against inside journal back, glue in place.

OVERHAND KNOT

Fabulous Frames

A supporting stand, a mat of color, a tender cradle, all describe the simple but intricate performance of a frame. A photograph without a frame lacks the architectural structure which holds it upright spotlighting smiling faces.

Frames are the perfect gift, whether for housewarming, a birthday or any occasion. I like to give frames to all my friends and family, particularly when I've taken a special photograph to place inside of it.

But mostly, I enjoy creating a one of a kind frame to compliment an extraordinary photograph. Unique frames really showcase your photos and make a statement of originality.

Suzanne

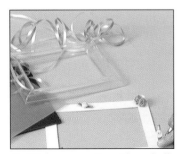

1 Fill frame cavity with embellishments. Secure with mat.

2 Assemble frame and insert photo.

Whether young or old, photographs of family and friends seem to delight the spirit. Display your photos in frames filled with ribbon, pompons, dried flowers and raffia.

Frames for All Ages

by Mike Kelly

MATERIALS: *Kelly's Crafts* Fill-It Frame, Mat, Assorted embellishments, Hot glue, Photo

INSTRUCTIONS:

Arrange or glue embellishments in frame cavity. Insert mat and photo in frame.

When you're wanted, they post your mug shot everywhere. You can hang mug shots at Grand Central Station...your kitchen.

Mug Shots
by Cyndi Hansen

MATERIALS: *Kelly's Crafts* Fun-Mugs, Assorted embellishments, Rick-rack, Decorative edge scissors, Stickers, Photos

1 Glue decorative paper to mug inserts. Add photos, embellishments, rick-rack and stickers.

2 Place insert between Clear and White sections of mug then snap together.

Celebration Candelarium
by Genevieve Neglia

MATERIALS: *Distlefink Designs* Deluxe Candelarium 51715, Wax crystals (Cornflower Blue 51210, Fluorescent Magenta 51276, Carnation Pink 51221), Balloon and star CandleStickers, 5" of wick, Photo, Curling ribbon, Party favors

INSTRUCTIONS:
Pour layers of wax crystals to form design. Insert wick and trim to ¼". Melt surface under a heat lamp to seal. Fill cylinder with photo, ribbon and party favors. Press CandleStickers on outside of cylinder. Place glass insert in cylinder.

1 Pour layers of wax crystals into glass insert.

2 Insert photo, ribbons and other embellishments in cylinder. Press balloon and star Candlestickers on cylinder.

3 Place insert in cylinder.

PATTERN
FOR
MIDDLE
LEFT
FRAME

PATTERN
FOR
TOP
RIGHT
FRAME

PERMISSION
is granted to photo-
copy patterns for
personal use.

PATTERN
FOR
BOTTOM
LEFT
FRAME

PATTERN
FOR
BOTTOM
RIGHT
FRAME

PATTERN
FOR
TOP
LEFT
FRAME
(copper
dabbed)

General Instructions. Use blue, red, purple or green clay. Paint frames with Turquoise and poly mix (equal parts), dab while wet with crumpled tissue. Let dry. Then dab with copper or paint trim gold.

Coiled Again

by Bridget Oas

MATERIALS: Oven bake clay, Straight cutting edge, Home oven, Baking sheet, White craft glue, Turquoise and Gold acrylic paint, Paintbrush, Craft knife

Frame. Roll ¼" diameter coils of oven bake polymer clay. Bend the coils into spirals to form the frame front. Cut photo opening and edges using a fine, straight craft knife. Outline photo opening with two coils of clay. Spaces between spirals can be filled with small balls of clay.

Backing & Spacers. Make a clay spiral ½" to 1" larger than photo opening. Cut off edges of spiral to form a rectangle. Wrap coils of clay around edges of rectangle. Cut a piece of coil the same length as bottom of backing and 2 small pieces of coil for spacers.

Stand. Form a spiral of clay coil making a long loop on the last wrap. Fill center of loop with a flattened clay ball or pieces of coil. Bend loop up at a 90° angle. Place a small ball of clay in bend to strengthen the stand.

Bake frame, backing, spacers and stand following manufacturer's instructions. Glue spacers to sides and bottom edges of backing. Glue backing on frame and stand on center of backing. Let dry flat. Paint frames as directed on page 36.

A crazy eight assortment of frames is sure to appeal to everyone in the family. With their simple style and easy assembly, these frames are made in a jiffy.

Crazy Eights Frames

by Bridget Oas

MATERIALS: *Crescent* smooth matboard, Tacky craft glue, Craft knife, Cutting board, Ruler, Pencil, Dimensional paint, Acrylic paint, Paintbrushes

Frame. Trace pattern and transfer to matboard using graphite paper. Cut out frame and center opening. Cut matboard from opening in half diagonally for stand. Draw arrow on back pointing to top of frame. Note: For frames with heavy designs or tiny beads, cut 2 frames (trim frayed edges with scissors), stack and glue together. Use Tacky craft glue for assembly.

Backing & Spacers. Cut backing piece 1" wider and 1" longer than photo opening. Mark top of backing. Cut four 1/4" wide spacers to fit sides of backing and 2 spacers 1/2" shorter than bottom of backing.

Backing. On back of frame, center backing over photo opening and trace around edges. Stack and glue 2 spacers just inside traced lines on sides and bottom. Glue backing on spacers.

Stand. Stack and glue stand pieces together. Apply glue to one short edge and press in place at center bottom of backing. To strengthen stand and backing, add a line of glue along sides and smooth with a strip of matboard.

RAISED DESIGN MIXTURE	DRYING TIME
6 teaspoons baking soda 3½ - 4 teaspoons acrylic paint Place ingredients in a cup to mix, then place mixture in an empty glue bottle.	Dimensional Craft Paint - 4 to 12 hours Mixture #1 - 12 hours Drying time depends on humidity and design size. A fan may be used to speed drying time.

Paint Olive Green rubbed with Gold for an antiqued look. Use brush handle to make design while wet.

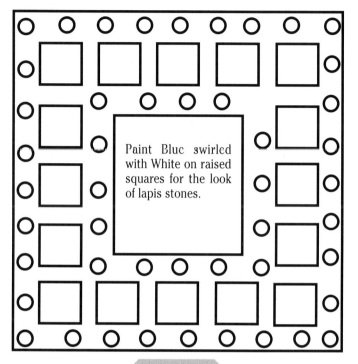

Paint Blue swirled with White on raised squares for the look of lapis stones.

Note: For silver frames, paint with 2 coats of Silver and polyurethane mix. Let dry between coats. Swirl on straight Silver lightly.

PERMISSION is granted to photo-copy patterns for personal use.

Paint with Silver for a pewter look.

Make oval from clay. Make indent for cabachon. Make design in clay. Bake and glue on. Paint with Silver, glue in cabachon.

Patterns for Frames on pages 38-39

RAISED DESIGNS

Materials: *Dimensional Mixture*, Empty glue bottle, Small paintbrush, Craft glue, Acrylic paint, Cup.

Design: Draw design lines on frame. Place frame on a cup so inner and outer edges do not touch the cup. Use *Dimensional Mixture* to make the raised design.

Hold bottle ½" to ¾" above frame and draw over design lines. If lines go to outer edge, continue over edge and let stream break off. Correct mistakes with a small paintbrush. When design is around photo opening, get as close to the edge as possible then use a small paintbrush to bring mixture flush with edge. Work from the inside of the opening. Let dry flat. If frame warps, turn over and press gently to flatten.

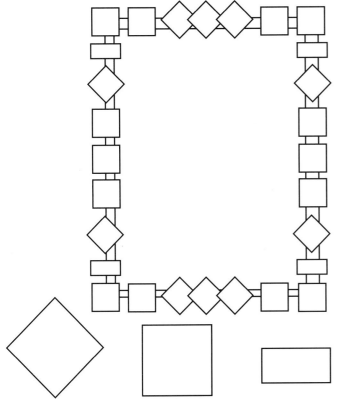

PATTERN PIECES & LAYOUT FOR BLACK GEOMETRIC FRAME
Cut pieces and assemble frame (see page 38 for placement). Glue on design pieces, let dry. Paint with 2 coats of Black and poly mix. Coat with poly for shine.

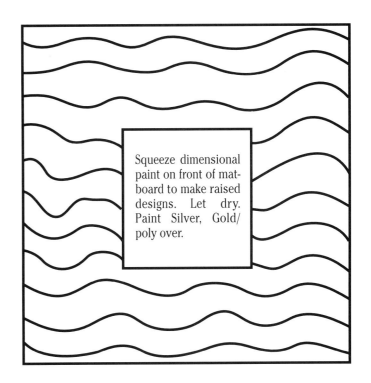

Squeeze dimensional paint on front of matboard to make raised designs. Let dry. Paint Silver, Gold/poly over.

Seeds

Seeds

Paint Silver basecoat. Paint outer triangles black and poly mix. Poly Black areas for extra shine. Use mustard seeds to fill inner triangles.

Seeds

Seeds

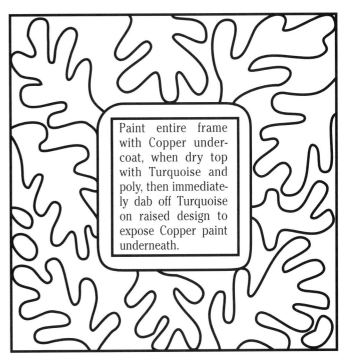

Paint entire frame with Copper undercoat, when dry top with Turquoise and poly, then immediately dab off Turquoise on raised design to expose Copper paint underneath.

Bear Hugs for our Cubbies

Families and Flowers Grow with Love, Faith and Hope

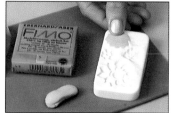

1 Soften clay following manu-facturer's instructions.

2 Press clay into push mold. Remove and bake.

3 Color baked pieces with Soft Tints paints or markers.

4 Or cut slices from a pre-formed clay cane. Bake.

5 Attach clay pieces to frame using GOOP glue.

Clay shapes mold together to form these picture perfect frames.

Appli-Clayed Frames

by Norma Jacobson

FAMILIES MATERIALS: *American Art & Clay Co.* FIMO (White, Green, Yellow), Sunflowers/Daisies Design Push Mold, Wood frame, Sheet of Clear plastic, White marker, GOOP glue, *Delta Soft Tints* paint (Brown, Green), Talcum powder, Baking sheet lined with parchment paper, Oven, Photo

BEAR HUGS MATERIALS: *American Art & Clay Co.* FIMO (Champagne), Teddy Bears Design Push Mold, Talcum powder, Divided wood frame, 12 glass seed beads, GOOP glue, White marker, *Delta Soft Tints* paints (Brown, Blue, Pink), Paintbrush, Baking sheet lined with parchment paper, Oven, Photos

PATCHES MATERIALS: *American Art & Clay Co.* Millefiori star patchwork square clay cane, Wood frame, Paper for mat, Scallop scissors, Photo

INSTRUCTIONS:
Soften clay. Dust molds with talcum powder and form clay pieces. Remove from molds.

Families Frame - Cut centers from 4 flowers. Bake. When cool, paint clay pieces referring to photo. Cut photos and circles of plastic to fit flowers. Arrange and glue on frame. Finish frame as shown.

Bear Frame - Mold bears, remove from mold and insert bead eyes. Bake. Paint clay pieces as shown. Finish frame as shown.

Patches Frame - Soften cane by pressing gently on all sides. Lengthen to 3" starting in center and working to ends. Cut 1/16" slices of cane. Bake. Arrange and glue on frame. Trim photo with decorative scissors, glue photo and caption on a colored paper mat. Insert photo.

Lettering diagrams on page 43

Bear Hugs for our Cubbies

Families and Flowers
Grow with Love,
Faith and Hope

PATTERN FOR
POINTILLISM FRAME
TOP LEFT PAGE 44

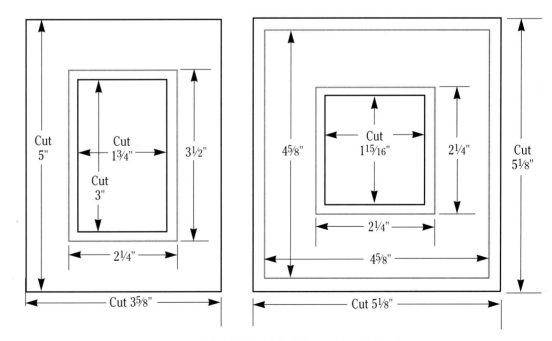

Cut 5"

Cut 1¾"

Cut 3"

3½"

2¼"

Cut 3⅝"

4⅝"

Cut 1¹⁵⁄₁₆"

2¼"

2¼"

4⅝"

2¼"

Cut 5⅛"

Cut 5⅛"

PATTERN AND DIMENSIONS FOR
"A POINT WELL TAKEN" FRAMES
ON PAGE 44

A Point Well Taken

by Bridget Oas

MATERIALS: *Crescent* Matboard frame, Paint pens, Acrylic paint, Polyurethane finish, Pencil, Tracing and transfer paper, Metal ruler

1 **Frame.** Assemble and paint frame Black following basic instructions on page 39. Add a small amount of water base polyurethane finish to basecoat paint. Paint frame front and back. Repeat if necessary for complete coverage.

2 **Trace Pattern.** Trace or measure pattern on page 43 and transfer to front of frame using white transfer paper.

3 **Design.** Outline designs with paint pen. Use a ruler to draw straight lines. Make dots with acrylic paint mixed with polyurethane finish using a small paintbrush handle. Note: Practice painting on a scrap of painted matboard until you are pleased with the effect.

Pattern for top left frame on page 43

1 Wipe slate with a damp cloth. Apply water base acrylic sealer to slate. Basecoat the background with White paint.

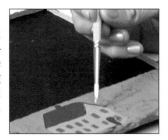

2 Trace and transfer pattern. Paint the scene referring to photo and using the listed paint colors

3 To antique, paint a wash of thinned Burnt Umber over the entire surface, wipe off excess with a dry cloth.

Folk Art plays on the heart with its sense of history, frugality and simplicity. Scenes on slates illustrate fond images of folk art crafts from centuries past. Paint a frame with pretty patterns for family and home.

Folk Heart Slate
by Virginia Pena

MATERIALS: *Cape Cod Cooperage* large rectangle slate frame, *Delta* acrylic paint (White, Antique Gold, Black, Sandstone, Burnt Umber, Dark Green, Barn Red), Water base sealer, Tracing and transfer paper, Paintbrushes

Instructions on page 47

PERMISSION
is granted to photo-
copy patterns for
personal use.

Folk Heart Slate

INSTRUCTIONS: Wipe slate with a damp cloth, let dry. Apply acrylic sealer.

Sky - White.

Grass - blend Pine Needle Green with Sandstone and Antique Gold.

Transfer pattern to slate.

House 1 - White.
  Roof - Black.
  Chimney - Barn Red.
  Door - Burnt Umber + Sandstone.

House 2 - Barn Red.
  Roof and windows - Black.
  Door - Burnt Umber + Sandstone.

House 3 - Antique Gold.
  Windows - Black.
  Door, roof and chimney - Barn Red.

House 4 - White.
  Roof and windows - Black.
  Door and chimney - Barn Red.

Birds - Black.

Tree trunks - Black + Burnt Umber.

Leaves - Pine Needle Green, Pine Needle Green + Antique Gold and Pine Needle Green + Burnt Umber.

Sheep - White.
  Legs and faces - Black.

Fence - Burnt Umber + Black.

Shadows - Pine Needle Green.

Apply sealer. To antique slate, use a damp cloth and rub Burnt Umber over surface. Wipe off excess immediately with a soft dry cloth. Seal.

There is no better way to brighten a room than with a fresh bouquet of flowers. Make every room delightful to the eye and soul with one of these floral frames.

Blooming Slates
Summer Bouquet

by Lauré Paillex

MATERIALS: *Cape Cod Cooperage* slate picture frame 202A, Acrylic varnish, Pencil and tracing paper, Stylus, Acrylic Extender, *DecoArt* acrylic paint (White, Antique Rose, Warm Neutral, Antique Gold, Victorian Blue, Black Plum, Antique Teal, Antique Maroon, Dusty Rose, Fleshtone), Paintbrushes

INSTRUCTIONS: Remove plexiglas insert and protect cardboard backing with plastic wrap. Wipe slate with a damp cloth, let dry.

Underpaint flowers and leaves - Warm Neutral. Let dry.

Leaves - Warm Neutral + Antique Teal allowing some White to show through. Float thinned Antique Teal + Black Plum along shaded edges. Center Vein - float Antique Teal + Black Plum.

Small Leaves - Warm Neutral + Antique Teal.

Daisy - White comma strokes. Centers - stipple Antique Gold, highlight White. Shade Antique Maroon. Float thinned Warm Neutral + Victorian Blue around shading.

Wild Rose - Antique Rose and White. Centers - stipple Antique Gold, highlight White. Shade Antique Maroon. Deepen shading with Antique Rose + Antique Maroon.

Morning Glory - White + Victorian Blue. Highlight White. Float center C strokes Victorian Blue + Black Plum. Dab with Antique Gold and Antique Rose.

Glaze - Moisten surface with extender. While still wet add Antique Gold to leaves and flowers. Antique Rose on edges of leaves, tips of daisy petals and flower centers. Victorian Blue with Black Plum shading on Blue flowers and buds. Dusty Rose around outside edge of frame. Varnish slate.

Pattern on page 50.

Instructions for Rose Slate Frame on page 51

1 Wipe slate clean. Paint slate with background color.

2 Paint design on slate following project instructions.

3 Highlight design and add details following project instructions

4 Spray frame with 2 coats of acrylic varnish.

A sunny afternoon walking along the beach in search of a grand conch shell is one of summer's great pleasures. A sail boat on the horizon and a lighthouse from days long ago make a memory of the ocean complete. Capture your favorite summertime memories on a special slate frame.

Suzy Sells Seashells by the Seashore
Memories for Sail
by Lauré Paillex

MATERIALS: *Cape Cod Cooperage* slate picture frame 204, Acrylic varnish, Pencil and tracing paper, Stylus, Acrylic extender, Paintbrushes, *DecoArt* acrylic paints (White, True Red, Black, Antique Gold, Victorian Blue, Light Cinnamon, Antique Teal, Cadmium Yellow)

1 Seal slate with White paint. Paint background.

2 Spray frame with 2 coats of acrylic varnish.

Instructions for frames on pages 52 and 53

PATTERN FOR "BLOOMING" SLATE
PHOTO PAGE 48

PERMISSION
is granted to photo-
copy patterns for
personal use.

Rose Slate Frame

by Virginia Pena

PAGE 48 PHOTO

MATERIALS: *Cape Cod Cooperage* oval slate frame, *Delta* Acrylic paint (White, Burnt Umber, Red Iron Oxide, Yellow, Antique Gold, Pine Needle Green), Water base sealer, Graphite transfer paper, Paintbrushes

INSTRUCTIONS: Wipe slate with a damp cloth, let dry. Apply acrylic sealer.

Front of slate - basecoat with two coats of White. Transfer pattern.

Roses - Red Iron Oxide C strokes, let dry. Pick up White on left and Red Iron Oxide on right, blend colors. Apply over rose shape.

Leaves - Pine Needle Green, Antique Gold and Pine Needle Green and Burnt Umber and Pine Needle Green.

Pollen - dots of Yellow.

Apply 2 coats of varnish.

PERMISSION is granted to photocopy patterns for personal use.

Memories for Sail

MATERIALS: on page 49

INSTRUCTIONS:

Remove plexiglas insert and protect cardboard backing with plastic wrap. Apply one coat of White paint, let dry.

Background - brush with White paint while wet pick up Victorian Blue and blend into wet White paint using light diagonal strokes.

Water - brush with thinned White paint. Blend Victorian Blue and touches of Antique Teal into waves.

Transfer pattern.

Sailboat - basecoat hull and roof with several coats of White.
Mast and Boom - Light Cinnamon.
Deck and cockpit - mix of White and Light Cinnamon + Victorian Blue.
Sails - shade with a mix of White and Light Cinnamon + Victorian Blue.
Man - Antique Gold, shade Light Cinnamon, highlight Cadmium Yellow.
Flag and detail line - True Red.

Channel Marker
Frame - True Red, shade True Red + Black.
Base - White + Black on top and Black + White on side.

Waves - White with extender.

Gulls - White, shade White + Black.
Feathers - Black + White.

Apply 2 coats of varnish.

PERMISSION is granted to photo-copy patterns for personal use.

Moonlight Sail
by Lauré Paillex
PAGE 49 PHOTO
MATERIALS: *Cape Cod Cooperage* slate frame, Acrylic varnish, Pencil and tracing paper, Stylus, White transfer paper, Acrylic Extender, Paintbrushes, *DecoArt* acrylic paint (White, True Red, Black, Antique Gold, Uniform Blue, Light Cinnamon, Antique Teal, Cadmium Yellow, Blush Flesh)
Instructions below:

INSTRUCTIONS:
Remove plexiglas insert and protect cardboard backing with plastic wrap.
Background - 2 coats of Uniform Blue.
Transfer pattern.
Sailboat
  Sails, hull and roof - basecoat White.
  Mast and boom - Light Cinnamon.
  Deck and cockpit - mix of White and Light Cinnamon + Uniform Blue.
  Sails - mix of White and Light Cinnamon + Uniform Blue.
  Man - Antique Gold, shade Light Cinnamon. Highlight Cadmium Yellow.
  Flag and detail line - True Red.
Water - brush with thinned White paint, blending in Uniform Blue.
  Add touches of Antique Teal in foreground.
  Waves - White with extender.
Lighthouse
  Tower - basecoat White, shade with mix of White + Uniform Blue.
  Roof - True Red, highlight White.
  Glass - wash White. Glaze Cadmium Yellow.
  Lamp - Antique Gold, highlight Cadmium Yellow. Tint Blush.
  Windows, railings and trim detail - Black.
  Beams of light - dry brush White then Cadmium Yellow.
Rocks - Black, Light Cinnamon and White using trowel knife.
Shrubs - stipple Cadmium Yellow and Antique Teal.
Apply 2 coats of varnish.

Wonderful Wood

Natural surfaces, sturdy textures and warm colors are desirable furnishings for a family room. The room where we relax in comfort with family and friends is the perfect setting for the things that remind us of loved ones from far and near.

The great room in my house is where the family has always gathered in the evenings and at holidays. A high ceiling with wood beams makes the oversize room inviting. Along the far wall where a staircase rises to the second floor, framed photographs record how all my children have grown from infants to adults.

Choosing wood frames of varying textures and sizes makes the photo wall an outstanding attraction. The collage of years and faces combine to make an imaginative family tree.

Suzanne

CHILDREN

Great Great Grandmother

TROUBLE

*E*ven one word can conjure impressive images. Simply said, the word 'Love' can change a picture into a treasure. Add your own words of wisdom to simple wood frames.

Simply Said

by Michelle Schmitz

MATERIALS FOR GRANDMOTHER: *Walnut Hollow* Weathered Gray Frame 64510, *Chart-Pak* letters, Photograph, Pre-cut double mat, Push points, Spray sealer, 5" x 7" piece of foamcore

MATERIALS FOR CHILDREN: *Walnut Hollow* Fresh Linen Frame 61510, *Chart-Pak* letters, Photograph, Pre-cut mat, Push points, Spray sealer, 5" x 7" piece of *Hunt* foamcore

MATERIALS FOR TROUBLE: *Walnut Hollow* Natural Pine Frame 62510, *Chart-Pak* letters, Photograph, Push points, Spray sealer, 5" x 7" piece of *Hunt* foamcore

INSTRUCTIONS: Following *Chart-Pak* instructions rub letters on frame. Spray with sealer to prevent damage to lettering. Insert pre-cut mat, photo and foamcore. Secure with push points.

1 Stain or paint frame if desired.

2 Rub letters on frame.

3 Spray frame with acrylic finish to seal.

1 Apply PeelnStick to wrong side of photo. Attach to posterboard.

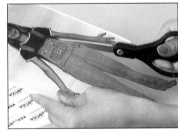

2 Cut photo apart at shoulders, knees, hips and elbows.

3 Make holes through photo with scissors, insert brads.

A marionette is the perfect actor for a stage show. Directed from behind the scenes, a string puppet lets a child act with spontaneous creativity. These photo jump-ups make the characters even more real when they are made with your own photographs.

Photo Jump-Ups
by Cyndi Hansen

MATERIALS: Enlarged color copy of a photo, Posterboard, *ThermOWeb* PeelnStick double sided adhesive, Brads, Scissors

INSTRUCTIONS: Apply Peel-n-Stick to wrong side of photo copy. Remove paper backing and stick photo copy on posterboard. Carefully cut out around subject photo. Cut photo apart at shoulders, elbows, hips and knees or as desired. Round off corners of each joint. Overlap two joints and use sharp point of scissors to make hole going through both layers. Insert brad through hole at front and bend brad to back. Repeat for each joint.

Cubicles

by Cyndi Hansen

MATERIALS: 3 copies of photos colored according to instructions on page 59, 3 *Design Originals 'Scrap Happy'* papers, *Woodworks* 2" wood blocks, Plaid Royal Coat Decoupage Finish, Sponge brush, Craft knife, Heavy rubber bands, Wax paper

INSTRUCTIONS:

Photos - Have photos enlarged to fit puzzles as follows: 2¼" x 6¼" for 3 standing blocks, 4¼" x 6¼" for 6 block puzzle and 6¼" x 8" for 12 block puzzle.

Blocks - Rubber band blocks together in groups of 3. Cover work area with wax paper. Use sponge to apply decoupage glue to top of one set of blocks. Align photo copy with edges of puzzle and smooth out bubbles with fingers. Allow to dry completely before going on to next step. Use craft knife to carefully trim excess photo from blocks. Remove rubber band and carefully cut each block apart. Repeat until all sets of blocks are glued and trimmed. Turn all blocks to the right and repeat using decorative paper. Continue until all sides of blocks are covered alternating paper with photo copies.

Seal - Apply decoupage glue with sponge brush. Dry completely and assemble.

Photo Tint Blocks

ADDITIONAL MATERIALS: Three *Woodworks* 2" wood blocks, Black and White color copies of photos, *Delta SoftTints* matte sealer, *Delta SoftTints*, Paintbrushes, Cotton swabs

INSTRUCTIONS: Seal each photo with matte sealer. Water down SoftTints and apply with a small soft brush. The color is transparent and will not be visible over Black. Apply as many coats as needed to obtain the desired color. Remove excess color with a cotton swab. Make blocks.

1 Glue photos and decorative paper on blocks. Trim excess.

2 Carefully cut blocks apart with a craft knife.

3 Sponge brush decoupage finish on blocks to seal.

CUBICLES PATTERN

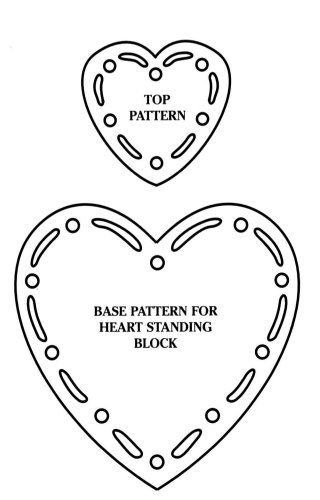

TOP PATTERN

BASE PATTERN FOR HEART STANDING BLOCK

Heart Standing Blocks

ADDITIONAL MATERIALS: *Woodworks* 3/8" x 3" wooden heart, 1/4" x 1 3/4" wood heart, 1/8" dowel rod, Three 2" wood blocks, *Design Originals 'Scrap Happy'* paper, Red, Green, and Cream acrylic paint, *DecoArt* transparent wash, Paintbrushes, Clear acrylic spray sealer, Spatter tool, Craft drill

INSTRUCTIONS: Drill holes through center of each block large enough for dowel rod. Drill hole in center of large heart and in end of small heart. Glue photos and paper to blocks. Cut paper apart. Paint front and back of each heart Red and sides Green. Wash Cream to lightly stain. Dot Cream on both sides of small heart and on top of large heart. Paint lines between dots. Spatter with thinned Cream. Spray hearts with sealer. Glue dowel in large heart. Thread blocks on dowel. Glue small heart on top.

Directions for Tinting Photos

Step 1. Copy photograph or art on a color copier set in the black/white mode. Note: in some cases this process actually improves faded or damaged photos or art.

Step 2. Seal the photo or art with *Delta SoftTints* matte sealer. Brush a smooth even coat of 'sealer' over the paper. It will curl up a bit but won't hurt. Dry 15 minutes.

Step 3. Tint paper copies with *Delta SoftTints*. Tints are a transparent paint medium. This enables you to paint right over the shadows and highlights of the paper copy and not cover them up. Use *SoftTints* in a watered down consistency. The best way is to pick up a tiny bit of paint on an artist brush, put this on a palette and add water to it so that it becomes a puddle of colored water. Work in a carefree manner remembering that *Tint* colors are transparent and will not be visible over black. Add more coats of color if desired. (Note: Remove excess color with a Q-tip.)

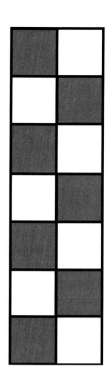

1 Sand box to remove rough areas.

2 Paint box desired color using a foam brush.

3 Paint metal or wood carving following instructions.

4 Glue carving to top of box with wood glue.

White & Gold Box

by Michelle Schmitz

MATERIALS: *Walnut Hollow* Recipe box 17280P and *Classic Dimension* wood carving 16402, 1" foam brush, Acrylic paint (Glorious Gold, Pale Yellow, Antique White), Decoupage finish, Four 3/8" wood screw plugs, 1/2" masking tape, Sandpaper, Wood glue, Spray finish, Photo copies, *Delta SoftTints* paints, small paint brush, *Chartpak* Rub-on letters, comb.

INSTRUCTIONS:

Basecoat entire surface Pale Yellow, let dry. Sand lightly. Repeat. Measure 1/2" around top of box and tape. Paint lid Antique White. Paint Glorious Gold checks. Paint bottom of box with a thick coat of Glorious Gold and comb. Paint wood carving Glorious Gold, let dry. Apply a light coat of Antique White, let dry. Remove tape. Sand lightly. Center photo copies on box and adhere with decoupage finish. Adhere Classic Dimension with wood glue. Rub on letters. Paint plugs Glorious Gold and glue on bottom of box. Spray entire box with finish.

Instructions for Red Box and Angel Box on page 63

See page 59 for instructions on photo tinting.

Knock on Wood

Faces Frame   (patterns are on page 131)

by Michelle Schmitz

MATERIALS: *Walnut Hollow* 53952 small frame clock, 1" foam brush, Graphite paper, Antique White and True Red acrylic paint, Fine sandpaper, Red and Black markers, *Backstreet Anita's* Water Clean Up Polyurethane

INSTRUCTIONS: Basecoat frame Antique White, let dry and sand. Repeat. Paint edge True Red. Transfer design. Trace over pattern with markers. Seal with polyurethane. Insert photo.

Safari Frame

by Pam Hammons

MATERIALS: *Walnut Hollow* 10" square frame, *Artifacts* 5 Leaf Spray Metal Carving, Safari clip art (page 63), Stylus, Wood stain. Acrylic spray finish, Green acrylic paint, White glue, Graphite paper

INSTRUCTIONS: Transfer design to frame and indent wood using a stylus. Apply stain and wipe off leaving stain in design. Trim clip art and glue in place. Paint metal carving Green, glue as shown. Spray frame with sealer.

Hand Frame

by Pam Hammons

MATERIALS: *Walnut Hollow* 9" x 12" frame, *JudiKins* Hand rubber stamp, Stamp pad, Stylus, Wood stain, Acrylic spray finish, White glue, Graphite paper

INSTRUCTIONS: Transfer design to frame and indent wood using a stylus. Apply stain and wipe off leaving stain in curves. Stamp hands as shown. Spray frame with sealer.

1 Make design on frame with a stylus.

2 Rub stain on frame using a soft cloth.

3 Spray acrylic finish on frame, let dry.

4 Stamp design on frame, or glue clip art designs on front of frame.

5 Spray with finish to seal and protect design.

Life is Full of Angels

Angel Box Art

PERMISSION
is granted to photo-
copy patterns for
personal use.

Red Box

PAGE 60 PHOTO

by Pam Hammons

MATERIALS: *Walnut Hollow* 5" x 8" wood box, *Artifacts* Laurel Wreath Metal Carving, Acrylic paint (Dark Red, Rose, Black, Green), Paintbrush, Sponge, White glue, Spray finish.

INSTRUCTIONS: Paint box Dark Red. Sponge lightly with Black and Rose. Paint metal carving leaves Green and bow Rose. Glue photo in center of box and metal carving on photo. Spray box with acrylic finish.

Angel Box

PAGE 60 PHOTO

by Pam Hammons

MATERIALS: *Walnut Hollow* 9" x 12" wood box, Color copy of album page, Paintbrush, Metallic Gold and Pink acrylic paint, Foam brush, Crackling medium, Spray acrylic sealer, White glue

INSTRUCTIONS: Paint box Gold, let dry. Paint Pink and apply crackling medium following manufacturer's instructions. Trim motifs from color copy of the angel and frame (see page 59 for photo tinting directions), glue on box lid. Spray with sealer.

PATTERNS FOR SAFARI FRAME

1 Cut out wood shapes using patterns.

2 Nail or glue shapes together following instructions.

3 Nail or glue frame pieces over photo.

Family rooms are in almost every home because they add a special place to gather each night. Many are decorated with photos that chronicle years of family activities. Capture your favorite family memories with just the right photo for this frame with a view.

Room with a View

by Delores Frantz

MATERIALS: Weathered wood (an old fence picket works great), 3/4" nails, Wood glue, 4" x 6" photo, Saw

INSTRUCTIONS: Following diagram cut frame pieces from wood. Place backs side-by-side with points together. Nail or glue braces across backs. Center house shape on base. Nail or glue base to house. Center roof pieces on top of house. Overlap longer piece over shorter piece at peak of house. Nail or glue. Center and glue picture to front of house. Nail or glue 1/2" frame pieces over edges of photo.

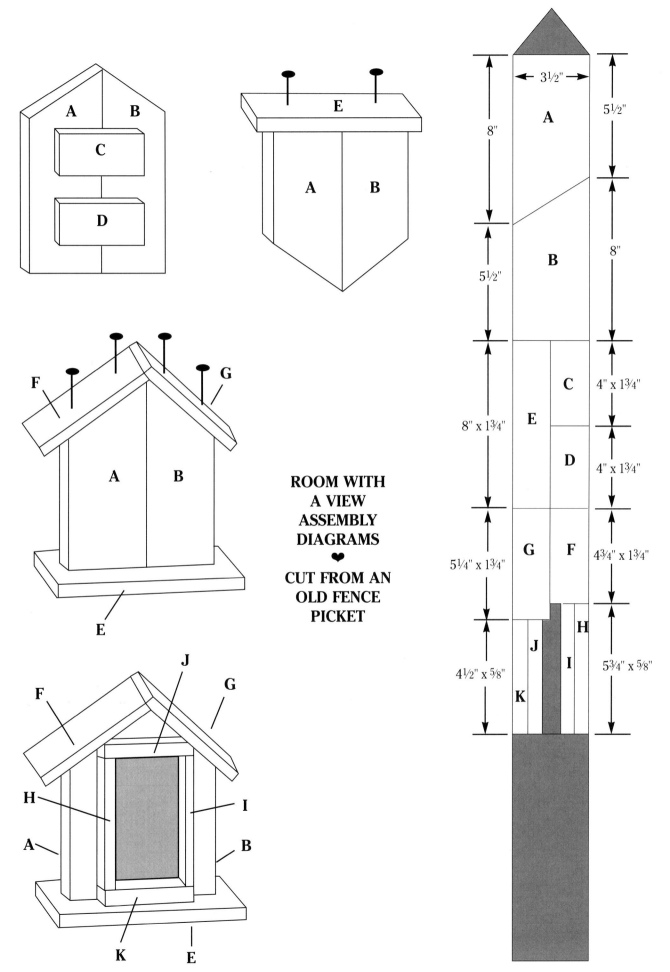

A B
C
D

E
A B

F
G
A B
E

ROOM WITH
A VIEW
ASSEMBLY
DIAGRAMS
♥
CUT FROM AN
OLD FENCE
PICKET

J
F
G
H
I
A
B
K
E

3½"
5½"

A

8"

B

8"

5½"

C   4" x 1¾"

E

D   4" x 1¾"

8" x 1¾"

G   F   4¾" x 1¾"

5¼" x 1¾"

J   H
I   5¾" x ⅝"

4½" x ⅝"

K

Small tin stars and animal shapes have traditionally been made as holiday ornaments to adorn trees and decorate houses. Punched tin shapes make a deeper impression when a photo is added.

Little Things Count

by Delores Frantz

MATERIALS: 26 gauge galvanized tin flashing, Burnt Umber acrylic paint, Matte acrylic spray finish, Denatured alcohol, Fine steel wool, 54" of Black 20 gauge wire, Newspaper, 3 photos, GOOP glue, Black permanent marker, Scallop edge scissors, Tin snips, Awl, Hammer, Metal file

INSTRUCTIONS:

Tin - Cut heart, tree, large star and 3 small stars from tin using tin snips. File points and edges smooth. Clean tin with alcohol. Sand with fine steel wool. Spray with clear acrylic.

Patterns - Tape pattern to tin shapes. Place shapes on a pad of newspaper. Use awl and hammer to punch holes. Remove pattern. Lightly hammer both sides to flatten shape and smooth edges around holes.

Paint - Paint tin and use a soft cloth to wipe off most of the paint. Spray with finish.

Photos - Cut small shapes from each photo, glue on large tin shapes.

Finish - Write year on small stars with marker. Cut wire into three 12" and three 6" pieces. Twist wire around a pencil. Leave 1" uncoiled at each end. Pull and stretch coils. Thread ends of a 12" wire through holes in large shapes. Bend a loop in wire ends. Press loop against back of shape. Attach small stars to large shapes in the same manner.

1 Cut shapes from tin using tin snips.

2 Punch holes with awl and hammer.

3 Paint tin and use a soft cloth to wipe off most of the paint.

4 For hanger, coil wire around a pencil.

LITTLE THINGS
COUNT SMALL
STAR PATTERN

LITTLE THINGS
COUNT LARGE
STAR PATTERN

PERMISSION
is granted to photo-
copy patterns for
personal use.

LITTLE THINGS
COUNT HEART
PATTERN

LITTLE THINGS
COUNT TREE
PATTERN

A portrait of Grandma in her wedding dress and a black and white photograph of Granddad in the army...These are pictures with history that we want to preserve for future generations.

Preserved for Posterity
by Carl Becker

MATERIALS: *Mill Store* wood albums, *EnviroTex* Lite®, Photos, Color clip art, Buttons, Permanent markers, Ribbon, Glitter, Gold cord, Acrylic paint, Paintbrushes

1 Sponge paint album cover front and back.

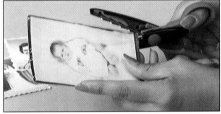

2 Trim photos using a pair of decorative edge scissors.

3 Arrange and glue photos and embellishments on front of album.

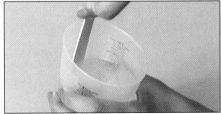

4 Mix *EnviroTex* following manufacturer's instructions.

5 Pour *EnviroTex* over entire album to seal embellishments.

Vacation Memories

Memories... They come from a wide variety of sources from vacations, to special occasions, to school days. What could be better than keeping these precious memories in an album made just for them.

Wooden It Be Wonderful?

by Carl Becker

BASIC MATERIALS: *Walnut Hollow* wood albums, *EnviroTex* Lite® Photos, Clip art, White craft glue

BASIC INSTRUCTIONS: Remove hardware from album. Paint front and back of album cover, let dry. Trim photos and clip art. Arrange and glue photos and clip art on album. Let dry. Mix *EnviroTex*® following manufacturer's instructions. Pour the mixture over entire album to seal the embellishments.

Train

MATERIALS: Train print fabric, Gold cord, Heavy weight paper

INSTRUCTIONS: Cut fabric to fit front of album with 1" extra on all sides to fold to inside. Thin craft glue and paint on front of album. Smooth fabric on glue, fold excess to inside and glue in place. Cut paper to cover edges of glued fabric, glue in place. Cut track pattern from fabric to fit album spine, glue in place. Trim and glue photos in train windows. Seal with *EnviroTex*®, let dry. Assemble album and tie cord through holes.

Off to School

MATERIALS: School clip art, Black round shoe lace, Red acrylic paint, Black fine tip permanent marker, Pencil

INSTRUCTIONS: Paint album Red, let dry. Cut out clip art and trim photo silhouettes to fit in bus windows. Arrange clip art, photos and pencil on album cover, glue in place. Write captions with marker. Seal with *EnviroTex*®, let dry. Assemble album and tie shoe lace through holes.

Graduation

MATERIALS: Brown wood stain, Black cord, Computer clip art

INSTRUCTIONS: Stain album, let dry. Trim photo corners and clip art. Arrange photo and clip art on album, glue in place. Let dry. Seal with *EnviroTex*®, let dry. Assemble album and tie cord through holes.

Vacation Memories

MATERIALS: Sky Blue and White acrylic paint, Sponge, Computer clip art, Gold dimensional paint.

INSTRUCTIONS: Paint album Blue and sponge White clouds, let dry. Trim photos and clip art. Arrange photos and clip art on album, glue in place. Outline captions with dimensional paint. Seal with *EnviroTex*®, let dry. Assemble album.

Paper Perfections

Photographs have become one of the most expressive means of sharing greetings throughout the year. For every occasion, there are cards with a border and photo window where a picture can slide in. The card becomes a gift in itself.

Handmade cards are easy to craft from fancy to simple paper supplies. Choosing just the right color or theme really makes a photograph stand out.

A paper photo mat, card or photo frame is the perfect embellishment to make your photograph a unique work of art.

Suzanne

BIRTHDAY GREETINGS

Thanksgiving Day

On this joyous feast day,
Happily we'll sing,
Giving thanks for all things
Which the harvests bring

Christmas Greetings

Seasons Greetings

your Christmas
happy one and the
Year full of joy

A Christmas Greeting With Best Wishes for the New Year

of the Red Lodge-Cooke City Road

From the days of pomp and circumstance, take a lesson in paper craft. A closer look will reveal the special techniques of rolling different shades of paper to make an exquisite impression when combined with photos.

A Time to Quill
by Delores Frantz

GENERAL MATERIALS: Needle tip quilling tool or hat pin, *Lake City* ⅛" x 23" quilling paper, White glue, Wax paper, Corrugated cardboard, Straight pins with round plastic heads, Masking tape, Ruler, Toothpicks, Tweezers

GENERAL INSTRUCTIONS:

Pattern - Tape pattern to cardboard. Cover pattern with wax paper and tape in place.

Paper - Measure correct amount of paper needed for a shape. Tear paper. The torn end is less noticeable when glued.

Rolling - Place paper end between thumb and index finger. Pinch paper end around tip of quilling tool. Roll paper without turning tool. Keep edges even. To make a tiny round center, roll the first portion of the coil tightly. Relax tension and roll remaining paper. Carefully slip coil off tool. Place coil on a flat surface and let it expand. Use a toothpick to place a tiny dot of glue on paper end. Press against the side of the coil.

Design - Make required quilled shapes and pin to cardboard using pattern as a guide for placement. Glue pieces together in sections. When all shapes are made, glue sections to backing. Tweezers are helpful when placing small pieces.

Quilling Shapes

Tight Roll - Roll paper tightly and glue before removing from tool.

Loose Roll - Roll coil, allow to expand and glue end to side of coil. This shape is the basis for many other shapes.

Teardrop - Make loose roll. Pinch together where end was glued.

Eye - Make loose roll. Pinch opposite sides leaving round center.

Holly - Pinch 6 points in loose roll with indentations between points.

Heart Scroll - Crease paper at center. Roll each end to fold.

Tendril - Roll strip with loose tension. Use tool to loosen roll forming a soft curl.

Ball Roll - Cut paper diagonally. Starting at the wide end, wind into a tight roll. The point should end at center of ball.

Bell - Carefully push center of tight roll out forming a bell shape.

Stem - Place a piece of paper on tool with thumb on top. Pull paper to curve slightly.

1 Measure the correct length of the paper and tear off.

2 Pinch paper strip around a quilling tool and roll without turning tool.

3 Pin quilled shapes and glue to mat using pattern as a guide.

4 Insert mat in frame. Tape photo on back of mat.

Christmas Photo

MATERIALS: 5" x 7" shadow box frame, White 5" x 7" mat with oval opening, *Lake City* (1 Gray, 10 Green, 2 Red, and 2 Metallic Gold strips of ⅛" quilling paper)

INSTRUCTIONS:

Shapes - Make the following shapes.

Wreath from 24 Heart Scrolls using 3" of Green paper each.

24 Scrolls using 2" of Green paper each.

24 Eyes using 2" of Green paper each.

Berries from 15 Ball Rolls using 2" of Red paper each.

3 Holly Leaves using 4" of Green paper each.

2 Bells using 23" of Metallic Gold paper each.

Clappers from 2 Ball Rolls using 2" of Gray paper each.

Glue wreath shapes around oval center of mat. Glue bells and holly to top of wreath. Place mat and picture in frame.

Wedding Photo

MATERIALS: 8" x 10" shadow box frame, Ivory 8" x 10" mat, Light Green 5" x 7" mat with oval center, Masking tape, *Lake City* (1 Yellow, 1 Red, 10 Purple, 8 Lavender, 7 Green, 3 Light Green, 4 White and 2 Pink strips of ⅛" quilling paper)

INSTRUCTIONS:

Shapes - Make the following shapes.

Violets

10 Teardrops using 4" of Purple paper each.

40 double rolled Loose Coils using 4" of Purple and 3½" of Lavender paper each.

10 open Hearts using 1" of Yellow paper each.

10 Tight Rolls using 1" of Red paper each.

Buds

9 double rolled Eye Coils using 4" of Pink and 3½" of Lavender paper each.

6 Eye Coils using 2" of Light Green paper each.

3 Curved Stems using 1½" of Light Green paper each.

Leaves

14 Teardrops using 4" of Green paper each.

Vines

Tendril using 10" of Green paper with coil on both ends.

Tendril using 8" of Green paper with coil on both ends.

Tendril using 4" of Green paper with coil on both ends.

Tendril using 4½" of Green paper.

Tendrils

9 Tendrils using 2" of Light Green paper each.

10 Tendrils using 1½" of Light Green paper each.

Sprays

44 Ball Rolls using 2" of White paper each.

4 Stems using 1" of Light Green paper each.

7 stems using 1½" of Light Green paper each.

Center 5" x 7" mat behind 8" x 10" mat and tape to secure. Place mats in frame. Glue vines and tendrils on mats. Glue 6 violets on top of vines. Glue 4 violets and 3 buds to mat. Glue leaves and sprays as shown. Place mat and picture in frame.

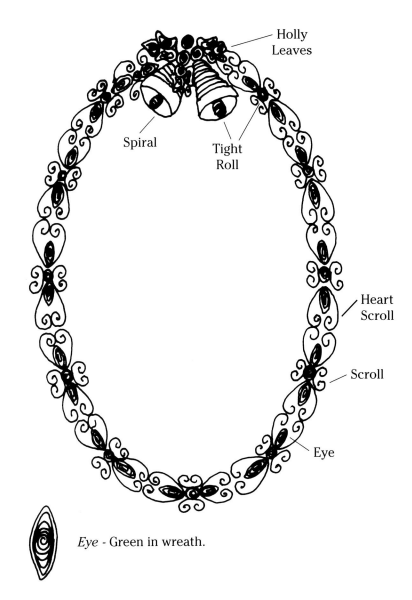

Eye - Green in wreath.

Tight Roll - Use Red for holly berry and Silver for bell clapper

Heart Scroll - Green for wreath.

Scroll - Green for wreath.

Holly leaves - Green.

Spiral - Silver for bells.

Double Loop
and Tight Roll
(centers of
flowers)

Tendrils

Tight Roll

Eye

Teardrop

Double
Teardrops

Teardrop - Purple flower petals.

Eye - Green bud leaves and lavender flower buds.

Tendrils - Green.

Double Teardrops - Green for leaves.

Double Loop - Yellow around flower centers.

Tight Roll - Yellow for flower centers
and White for berries on tendrils.

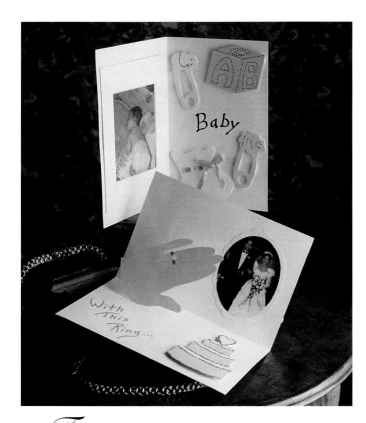

The beary cutest cards are often to die for. A few words and simple shapes made from colored paper can express greetings on their own.

To Die For

by Barbara Warnix Boyd

WEDDING CARD MATERIALS: *Crafty Cutter* Die Cuts (wedding rings, hand with ring, wedding cake), Pop-up sticky adhesive dots, Fine Gold glitter, Glitter glue, Gold paint pen, Square White paper doily, Wedding photo, $8\frac{1}{2}$" x 11" sheet of Gold paper, $8\frac{1}{2}$" x 11" sheet of cardstock, 8" x 5" piece of Pink paper trimmed with deckle edge scissors, Craft knife

INSTRUCTIONS:

Outer Card - Score and fold Gold paper in half to form card. Glue Pink paper on front. Cut doily in half diagonally and fold each piece as shown in diagram. Cut off pointed tip of each piece, fold edge under. Mount on front of card as shown. Mount wedding rings using adhesive dots.

Inner Card - Score and fold card stock in half. With craft knife make two lengthwise 3" slits $\frac{1}{2}$" apart and 2" from left edge of paper. Center slits between top and bottom of page. Make a straight scored line at top and bottom between slits. Fold away from card so paper piece pops out when card is open at a 45° angle. Mount hand on front of piece. Mount wedding cake with adhesive dots. Write message with Gold pen. Glue cards together and photo in place.

BABY CARD MATERIALS: Bear die cut, $8\frac{1}{2}$" x 11" sheet of cardstock, Small pieces of Black and Red paper, 12" of $\frac{1}{4}$" ribbon, Black calligraphy pen, Pop-up adhesive dots

INSTRUCTIONS: Score and fold cardstock in half to make card. Place small pieces of Black paper behind ear and nose openings of bear die cut and use a piece of Red paper for heart. Mount die cut on front of card using adhesive dots. Make eyes on card behind die cut with a Black pen. Mount remaining baby die cuts on inside of card using adhesive dots. Run a piece of ribbon through holes in bootie die cut and tie in a bow. Write words with pen.

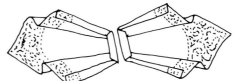

Folding diagram shown from back.

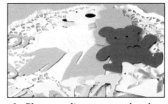

1 Choose die cuts and other supplies for card.

2 Glue embellishments and die cuts on front of card.

3 Glue remaining die cuts inside card.

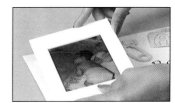

4 Glue photo in place and write message.

Thirsting for a refreshing craft? You'll get creative with Pergamano *paper. An enjoyable afternoon can be spent embossing designs on special paper to make elegant cards.*

We're Parched for Paper

by Mary Oskamp

MATERIALS: *Pergamano* paper, Perga-Kit, White paper, Tinta ink, Pintura paint, Embossing tools, Perforating tools, Parchment scissors, Felt pad

Christmas Window Card

MATERIALS: Gold, Green, Red, and White Tinta ink, Red, Green, Yellow and Brown Pintura paint, 1101 medium and 1102 large embossing tools, 1106 two needle, 1105 four needle, Semicircular and 1111 flower perforating tools

INSTRUCTIONS: Trace pattern using ink colors shown in photo. Paint. To emboss, use large tool for window, curtains, panes and snow. Use medium tool for ribbon, berries and leaves. Place on pad and perforate border design with 4 needle tool. Use semicircular tool just outside curtain line. Make flowers from back. Use 2 needle tool to make holes around window panes. Cut 4 hole perforations from hole to hole to make a + design. Cut and fold White paper to make inner card. Glue photo on inner card, insert in card.

Heart Frame Card

MATERIALS: Pink and Green Pintura paint, Gold and White Tinta ink, 1106 two needle perforating tool, Decorative scissors

INSTRUCTIONS: Trace pattern using ink colors shown in photo. Color flowers and leaves. Use 2 needle tool to perforate opening around inside edge of heart. Fold card, cut edges with decorative scissors, outline Gold. Cut and fold White paper to make inner card. Glue photo on inner card, insert in card.

Oval Frame Card

MATERIALS: White Tinta ink, Pink Dorso pastel color, 1101 embossing tool, 1106 two needle and 1111 flower perforating tools

INSTRUCTIONS: Trace pattern using White ink. Shade edges with pastel color. Perforate flowers from back and use 2 needle tool around edge of oval. Cut out oval inside perforations. Fold card, perforate edge with 2 needle tool. Glue photo on inside card, insert in card.

1 Trace pattern on *Pergomano* paper using inks.

2 Color designs referring to photos.

3 Perforate designs using needle tools listed in instructions.

4 Cut around perforations to make edge designs.

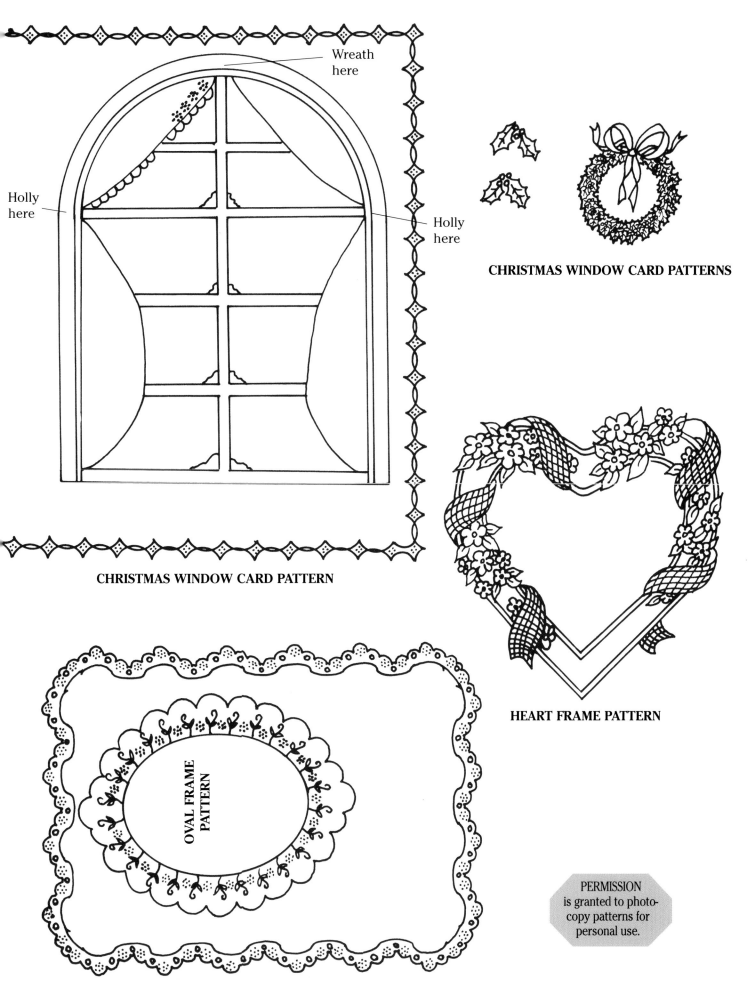

Wreath
here

Holly
here

Holly
here

CHRISTMAS WINDOW CARD PATTERNS

CHRISTMAS WINDOW CARD PATTERN

HEART FRAME PATTERN

OVAL FRAME PATTERN

PERMISSION
is granted to photo-
copy patterns for
personal use.

Embossing

1 Place stencil on wrong side of paper and emboss design.

2 Color designs with ink, *Paintstiks*, chalk or acrylic paint.

3 Add glitter to embossed designs.

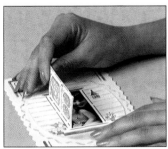

4 Cut opening and glue photo in place.

Every detail is intricately planned for a special occasion like a wedding or an anniversary. First impressions can lead to a 'yes' or 'no', so make a deep impression with a beautifully embossed invitation. You are sure to get the answer you want.

By Invitation Only

MATERIALS: *American Traditional Stencils* Stencil brushes, Embossing tool, Light table, Colors (ink, *Paintstiks*, chalk, acrylics), Decorative scissors, Embossing powders, Glitter, Craft knife, Scissors, Glue, Masking tape, Handmade papers, Assorted trims, Photos, Heat gun (for embossing powders)

GENERAL EMBOSSING INSTRUCTIONS: Tape brass stencil to a light table with masking tape. Tape paper face down over the stencil. Use the embossing tool tip to draw inside every design of the brass stencil on the back of the paper. Remove all tape to see the embossed design on the front.

Open Door

MATERIALS: *American Traditional Stencils* (GS-125 Screen Door, BL-477 Oval Cameo Frame, FS-844 Ivy), 4" x 5" piece of Canson self adhesive paper

INSTRUCTIONS: Emboss oval on paper. Cut out oval. Stencil door in center of oval. Use a 1" x 5" strip of paper to stencil clapboards. Add lantern, ivy and flower pot. Color as shown. Cut door open. Add photo behind door using self stick paper.

Heart Card

MATERIALS: *American Traditional Stencils* (BL-136 Heart), 4" canvas coaster, Stick and Hold adhesive backing, High gloss varnish

INSTRUCTIONS: Stencil heart in center of canvas Red, tint with Blue. Varnish canvas. Apply adhesive to back and cut around border of heart $1/8$" from edge. Peel off backing and attach heart to card.

Gold Embossed Frame

MATERIALS: *American Traditional Stencils* (GS-118 Oval Frame) $3^{1}/_{2}$" x 5" piece of Gold foil paper

INSTRUCTIONS: Trim paper with decorative scissors. Emboss oval, scroll, frame and two matching edges in center of paper. Remove stencil and reposition for other border edges. Cut out center of oval and insert photo. Attach gold foil to a card.

Rosewood Frame

MATERIALS: *American Traditional Stencils* (GS-121 Rosewood Frame and FS-805 Hearts), 5" x 6" piece of Green and Gold marbled paper, $3^{1}/_{2}$" x $4^{1}/_{2}$" piece of White cardstock, $4^{1}/_{2}$" of $5/8$" Gold ribbon

INSTRUCTIONS: Trim papers with decorative scissors. Stencil frame in center of cardstock, add embossing powder, remove excess and heat. Cut out center of frame. Stencil hearts and emboss with powder. Cut out. Glue ribbon diagonally across top right corner of Green paper, trim. Attach photo and glue hearts in place.

The truth be told, stories about people, places and things of the past are what make this attractive album so interesting.

An Old Ivy Tale

by Barbara E. Swanson

MATERIALS: *Mill Store* wood album, *American Traditional Stencils* (Bl676 Scroll, Bl-926 Berry & Vine, BL-477 Oval Cameo Frame and GS-118 Oval Frame), Acrylic paint (Green Mist, Antique Teal, Alizarin Crimson, Metallic Gold, Metallic Silver), Clear art glaze, Wood sealer, Paint and stencil brushes, Sea sponge, Parchment pages for album, White watercolor paper, Assorted handmade papers, Matte spray sealer, Glue pen

Album Cover INSTRUCTIONS: Remove posts and hinges from wood album. Seal front and back covers, let dry. Seal inner covers and edges. Lightly sand to smooth. Paint covers with 2 coats of Green Mist. Mix art glaze with Antique Teal following manufacturer's instructions. Brush on outer covers. While still wet, pounce lightly with a damp sponge. Then pounce with crumpled plastic wrap for a fine grained leather look. Repeat on inside of covers. With right sides up, place sections side by side on flat surface, tape together on back. Referring to photo, stencil Berry & Vine on covers using Silver, Gold and Crimson paints. Let dry. Spray with sealer and reassemble album.

Album Pages

Decorate pages with handmade papers, stenciled frames and stenciled borders for a look of elegance.

1 Paint album cover and stencil with berry and vine design.

2 Stencil designs on parchment paper for album pages.

3 Cut out stenciled designs and arrange on album page.

4 Glue designs, frames and photos in place on pages.

Roses are red, violets are blue. What better way to save your treasures than to keep them in an album made by you.

Roses are Red   *by Barbara E. Swanson*

MATERIALS: *Accent* 7" x 9" handmade paper diary, *American Traditional Stencils* (Trousseau BL-556, Ivy BL-483, Scroll BL-676, Cameo Trims BL-122, Simple Edges BL-634, Scroll Frame F5-948), Two lace motifs, Sea sponge, Mauve, Light Green and Light Blue acrylic paint, 1 yard of ⅜" Blue satin ribbon, Piece of watercolor paper, Mulberry paper or Assorted handmade papers, *Creative Art Products Shiva* Artist's Paintstiks (Azo Yellow, Napthol Red, Prussian Blue, Sap Green), Stencil brushes, *Zig* Two-Way Glue pen, *Zig* Black fine-line marker, Craft knife

GENERAL INSTRUCTIONS:

1. Paintstiks are self sealing and may have a thin "skin" on them. Simply rub away this skin to expose fresh paint. Swirl a separate circle / layer of each color of paint onto a paper plate as your palette. Set Paintstiks aside until additional paint is required.   2. To stencil, dab the end of a dry brush lightly onto paint. Pounch bristles onto a paper towel to remove excess paint. There should be very little paint on the brush. Pounch, or swirl brush over stencil openings. Using one brush for each color of paint, stencil each design with the lightest color (Azo Yellow) first and end with the darkest color (Sap Green). These paints blend beautifully so don't be afraid to overlap colors. It will add beauty to the finished project.   3. Mask out any portions of the stencil not used with masking tape. The reverse side of a stencil can be used to create mirror images.   4. To fray the edges of the Mulberry paper, slightly dampen the edges and gently pull.

Album Cover - Lightly sponge front and back covers of album Light Blue. Glue ribbon around center of album leaving ends free. Fray Mulberry handmade paper and glue on front. Glue lace on paper. Stencil rose on watercolor paper coloring with Paintstiks. Outline with the fine-line black marker. Cut out design and glue on lace.

Album Pages

Sponge pages or glue on handmade paper. Add ribbon and lace. Stencil watercolor paper for frames and corners.

1 Stencil designs on handmade paper for album pages.

2 Stencil frame and corner designs on watercolor paper.

3 Glue photos in frames and frames on page.

Album pages are filled with the memories of our lives. Make them even more special by adding paper backgrounds and embellishments.

Vintage Album Pages

MATERIALS: Album pages, *Artifacts* Paper doilies (white and gold), Paper ribbon, *Artifacts* Victorian motifs, Colored papers, Decorative edge scissors, *Zig* Two-Way Glue pen

INSTRUCTIONS: Cut mats and frames from papers. Trim papers and photos with decorative scissors. Arrange photos on page. Add motifs and paper ribbon.

1 Cut out the designs from Victorian motif papers.

2 Cut frames and corners from Gold paper doilies.

3 Trim photos and glue inside the frames. Glue photos on the pages.

SCHOOL DAYS

BUS

My Cat

A furry companion is frequently seen in family photographs and often has a few photos of his own. Make the perfect mat to frame one of the most important members of the family.

A Matter of Photographs *by Cyndi Hansen*

MATERIALS: Photos, Black fine-line marker, Colored pencils, White eraser, Clear acrylic sealer, Craft knife

MATERIALS FOR DOG & CAT: 8 x 10" Frame

MATERIALS FOR SCHOOL: *Hunt* Foamcore (two 13 x 15" pieces), Saw, Sandpaper, 2 yardsticks ($1^1/_8$" wide), Tacky glue, Hot glue

BASIC INSTRUCTIONS FOR MAT:
Trace and transfer design onto Bristol board or cardstock. Outline design with Black marker. Use a craft knife to cut out openings for photos. Color design with colored pencils working from top to bottom or left to right so as not to smudge design. Blow off excess color as needed and rub off mistakes with a White eraser. Seal design with 2 light coats of sealer, allow to dry.

Dog & Cat - Trace, cut and color an 8 x 10" mat.
Tape photos to back of mat and secure in frame.

School - Trace, cut and color a 13 x 15"mat.
For frame front, use a ruler to draw lines 1" from each edge of one piece of foamcore. Cut out the center. Use a saw to cut two $15^1/_8$" and two $10^7/_8$" pieces from yardsticks. Smooth edges with sandpaper. Tacky glue yardstick pieces to foamcore allowing edges to overhang. Let dry. Tape photos to ba ck of mat and secure in frame. Glue remaining piece of foam core to back.

See patterns on pages 92-95.

1 Cut openings for photos using a craft knife.

2 Color design working from top to bottom or from left to right.

3 Draw lines 1" from edge of foamcore. Cut out the center.

4 Cut yardsticks and glue on foamcore base.

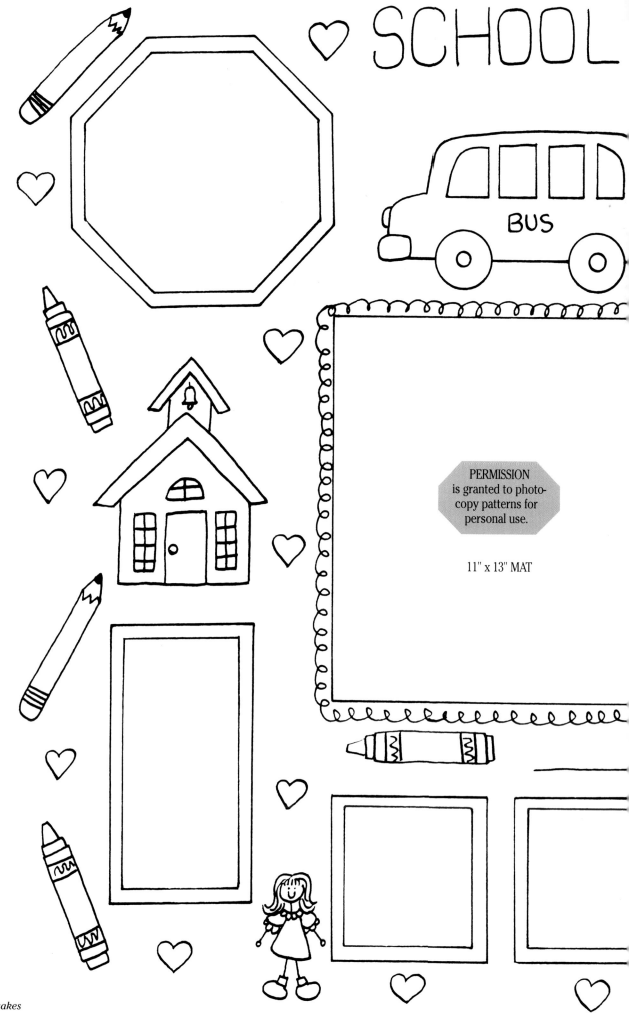

SCHOOL

BUS

PERMISSION
is granted to photo-
copy patterns for
personal use.

11" x 13" MAT

DAYS

PERMISSION is granted to photo-copy patterns for personal use.

8" x 10" MAT

PERMISSION
is granted to photo-
copy patterns for
personal use.

8" x 10" MAT

When that special day approaches for celebrating the long lasting love our parents have given us, we find ourselves among the mob of wild-eyed shoppers progressing from shop to shop seeking just the right thank you. Make extra special Mothers' and Fathers' Day gifts with these one of a kind photo mats.

Familiar Faces

by Cyndi Hansen

MATERIALS: 8 x 10" Frame, Photos, Colored pencils, White eraser, Clear acrylic sealer, Craft knife, Black fine-tip permanent marker

INSTRUCTIONS:
Trace and transfer design onto Bristol board or cardstock. Outline design with Black marker. Use a craft knife to cut out openings for photos. Color design with colored pencils working from top to bottom or left to right so as not to smudge design. Blow off excess color as needed and rub off mistakes with a White eraser. Seal design with 2 light coats of sealer, allow to dry. Tape photos to back of mat and secure in frame.

See patterns on pages 98-99.

No other moment in life can match the first time you see a new baby's face. It fills the heart with emotion and there is no denying the urge to tell everyone you see that there is a new baby in the family. Make the moment last with a picture perfect setting.

It's a Boy, It's a Girl
by Cyndi Hansen

MATERIALS: 8 x 10" Frame, Photos, Birth Announcements, Colored pencils, White eraser, Clear acrylic sealer, Craft knife, Black fine-tip permanent marker

INSTRUCTIONS:
Trace and transfer design onto Bristol board or cardstock. Outline design with Black fine-tip permanent marker. Use a craft knife to cut out openings for photos. Color design with colored pencils working from top to bottom or left to right so as not to smudge design. Blow off excess color as needed and rub off mistakes with a White eraser. Seal design with 2 light coats of sealer, allow to dry. Tape photos to back of mat and secure in frame.

See patterns on pages 100-101.

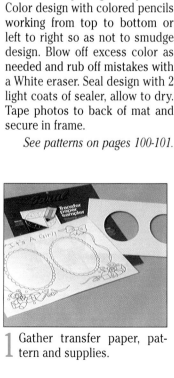

1 Gather transfer paper, pattern and supplies.

2 Trace design and transfer to Bristol board or cardstock.

3 Outline design with Black permanent fine-tip marker.

4 Color design working from top to bottom or left to right..

PERMISSION
is granted to photo-
copy patterns for
personal use.

8" x 10" MAT

Mommy
and
Me

PERMISSION
is granted to photo-
copy patterns for
personal use.

8" x 10" MAT

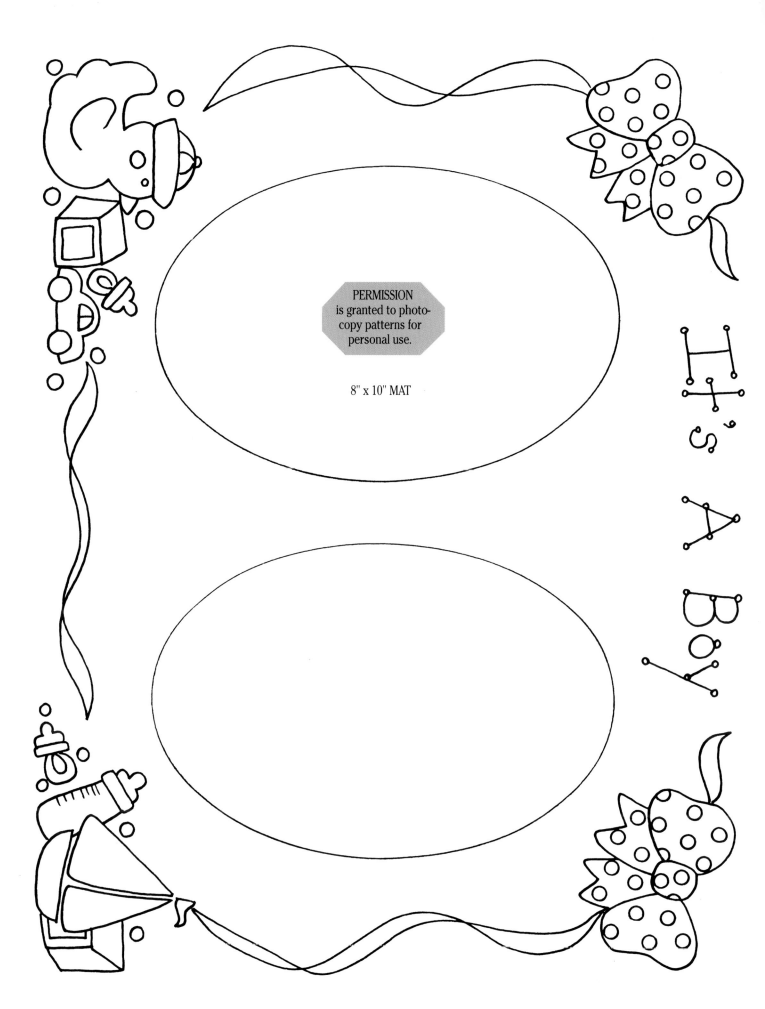

PERMISSION
is granted to photo-
copy patterns for
personal use.

8" x 10" MAT

It's A Boy

It's A Girl!!

PERMISSION is granted to photo-copy patterns for personal use.

8" x 10" MAT

Favorite Fabrics

An ordinary article of home decor, like a throw pillow, serves as one of the home's most comforting furnishings. Indescribably soft and cuddly, a sofa pillow is the first thing you reach for when settling down for a good movie or a night of relaxing family time.

With a fabric covering, a pillow is not only nice to hold, but also an attractive piece to use for home decoration. Fabric covering with custom designs are especially complementary.

Think also of photographs that can be transferred to fabric. Make a perfect pillow, wall hanging or vest to wear. The possibilities with fabric and photographs are endless.

Suzanne

Scrapbooks hold special keepsakes, pictures and mementos capturing the best of your memories. Make every day an occasion to rediscover your favorite time by reproducing scrapbook pages on fluffy pillows.

Stuffed with Pride
by Paula Gentile

MATERIALS: 12" pillows, Scrapbook square album pages, *Hues Photo Effects* iron-on transfer paper, 9 x 9" Muslin for transfers, *La Mode 'Remember When'* embellishments, Jewel glue, Assorted Ribbon and Lace

INSTRUCTIONS: Use a color copy machine to copy photo album pages onto *Photo Effects* transfer paper (reduce the page size to 8 x 8"). Transfer photocopy to muslin fabric with a home iron (see manufacturer's instructions).

Trim fabric edges and finger press a narrow hem. Pin fabric in center of pillow and slip stitch in place. Sew ribbon, lace or braid around edge of fabric. Glue embellishments in place.

1 Transfer the photocopy to muslin fabric with an iron.

2 Turn edges of muslin under and pin fabric on pillow.

3 Choose embellishments. Sew or glue to pillow.

It is nice to be surrounded by family year round. Make a great addition to any room with this wonderful family photo holder.

A Family Affair
by Cyndi Hansen

MATERIALS: 6 photos, *Hues Photo Effects* iron-on transfer paper, 1/2 yard of Muslin for transfers, Fabric for photo backgrounds, 2" x 12" piece of muslin for wording, 2¼" x 12½" and 2½" x 13" piece of fabric for wording background, Printed Fabrics (7" square of fabric for photo mats, Two 4½" x 13½" pieces of fabric for pockets, Two 14" x 17½" pieces of fabric for wall hanging, three 1 x 12" pieces of fabric for bows), 14" x 17½" piece of quilt batting, Heavy-weight paper-backed fusible web, 10 wood buttons, Ten ⅜" buttons, Acrylic paint, Paintbrush, Embroidery floss, Pinking shears, Decorative edge scissors, Black permanent marker

INSTRUCTIONS:

Transfers - Use a color copy machine to copy photos onto *Photo Effects* transfer paper. Trim photos, transfer to muslin with a home iron (see manufacturer's instructions). Fuse web to wrong side of transfers. Trim transfer and fuse to background fabric. Note: Cover transfers before ironing. Fuse web to wrong side of background fabric. Trim fabric to desired sizes. Fuse pieces to pockets using photo as a guide. Pink edges of each pocket piece. Write words with marker. Fuse web to wrong side of muslin and to background fabrics. Remove paper backing and layer fabrics. Place on wall hanging front, fuse in place.

Wall Hanging - Pin pocket pieces to front of wall hanging. Layer wall hanging front, batting, and back, pin. Cut three 1" x 12" fabric strips with pinking shears. Tie each strip into a bow, trim ends. Pin bows to top of wall hanging. Sew around wall hanging ⅝" from edge catching ends of bows in stitching. Sew along sides and bottom of each pocket and between transfers. Pink edges of wall hanging.

Buttons - Paint buttons, allow to dry. Sew buttons to wall hanging as shown in photo.

1 Iron each photo transfer on a muslin square.

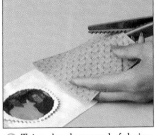

2 Trim background fabrics to desired size.

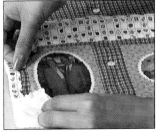

3 Fuse photos and background fabrics in place.

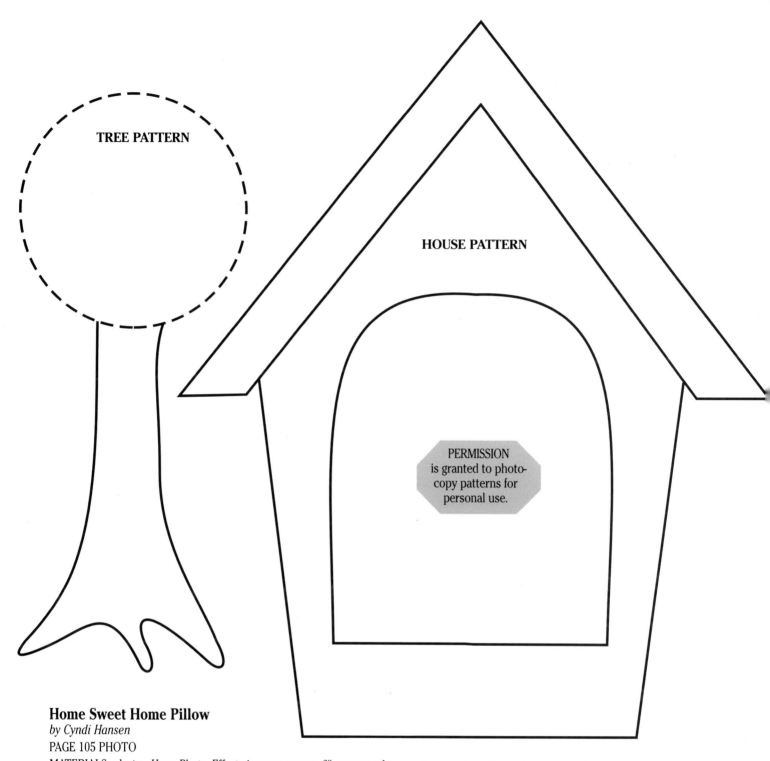

TREE PATTERN

HOUSE PATTERN

PERMISSION
is granted to photo-
copy patterns for
personal use.

Home Sweet Home Pillow
by Cyndi Hansen
PAGE 105 PHOTO

MATERIALS: photo, *Hues Photo Effects* iron-on paper, 6" square of Muslin for transfer, 9" square of muslin for center, 13" fabric square for pillow front, 9½" x 13" and 6½" x 13" pieces of fabric for pillow back, Fabrics for appliques, 12" pillow form, Four ¾" buttons, Paper-backed fusible web, Embroidery floss, 1 yard of jute, Black fine-point permanent marker, Hot glue

INSTRUCTIONS:

Transfers - Use a color copy machine to copy photo onto *Photo Effects* transfer paper. Trim photo and transfer to muslin with a home iron (see manufacturer's instructions).

Following manufacturer's instructions, fuse web to wrong side of muslin piece. Trace patterns on paper backing side of web spacing at least 1" apart, cut apart. Fuse patterns to wrong side of applique fabrics and cut out appliques. Fray edges of muslin center. Remove paper backing. Arrange appliques and photo transfer on muslin cen-

ter. Iron in place. Note: Cover transfer before ironing in place.

Yo-yo - Cut a 5¼" circle from fabric. Fold raw edge ⅛" to wrong side and baste close to folded edge. Pull thread to gather tightly. Flatten circle with gathers at front,. Run needle to back and knot thread. Sew yo-yo to top of tree trunk.

Center Piece - Write words with marker. Pin center piece to center of pillow front. Using embroidery floss and a running stitch, sew in place. Sew one button on each corner.

Pillow - Press one short side of each back piece ½" to wrong side. Matching right sides, raw edges and overlapping folded edges of back pieces, pin pillow back to pillow front. Sew around edge of pillow using a ½" seam allowance. Turn pillow right side out and stuff.

Tassels - Cut five 8" pieces of jute. For each tassel, unravel one piece. Hold lengths together and fold in half. Wrap a piece of unraveled jute around tassel ½" from top, tie in back. Sew tassels on corners.

ustomize a picture pillow for any sofa, chair or day bed. Choose a trim and fabric to match, then simply transfer your favorite photograph. It will make a sensational statement!

A Family Affair *by Cyndi Hansen*

School Pillow

MATERIALS: 4" x 5½" photo, 5½" x 5½" artwork, *Hues Photo Effects* iron-on transfer paper, 13" square of Muslin for transfers, 13" fabric square for pillow front, 9½" x 13" and 6½" x 13" pieces of fabric for pillow back, 4 yards of 4" width fabric for ruffle, 12" pillow form, *Wright's* Red, Green and Yellow jumbo rick rack, 4 each of Red, Green and Yellow ¾" buttons, Paper-backed fusible web, Fabric for appliques, Hot glue

INSTRUCTIONS:

Transfers - Use a color copy machine to copy photos and artwork onto *Photo Effects* transfer paper. Transfer photo and artwork to muslin with a home iron (see manufacturer's instructions) spacing designs at least 2" apart. Cut out photos and artwork. Following manufacturer's instructions, fuse web to wrong side of muslin pieces. Fuse web to wrong side of applique fabrics. Cut applique fabrics to desired shapes.

Pillow Front - Remove paper backing from web. Place transfers and appliques on the front of a 13" square of fabric. Iron in place. Note: Cover transfer before ironing in place. Pin rick rack around transfers. Sew in place.   Ruffle - With wrong sides together, fold 4" fabric in half and baste to gather. Matching raw edges, pin ruffle to pillow front rounding at corners. Baste in place.

Pillow Back - Press one short side of each back piece ½" to wrong side. Matching right sides and raw edges and overlapping back pieces, pin pillow back to pillow front. Sew around edge of pillow using a ½" seam allowance. Remove basting threads and clip corners. Turn pillow right side out and stuff.

Finish - Glue buttons to corners of rick rack squares.

1 To make yo-yos, fold fabric under ⅛", sew around edge.

2 Pull stitches tight, push needle through center and tie off.

3 For tassels, unravel 8" pieces of jute.

4 Separate one strand of jute to tie off tassel.

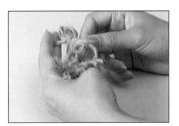

5 Fold unravelled jute in half, tie off with a jute strand.

6 Trim tassels and sew on corners of pillow.

Bloom where You're Planted!

Plant a seed and watch it grow. Sunflowers really make the scene with big bold blossoms. You'll love this bright set of blooming accents that bring cheer all year round.

Bloom Where You're Planted
by Cyndi Hansen

Personalized Doll

MATERIALS: color photo of a face, *Hues Photo Effects* iron-on transfer paper, Premade 12" stuffed doll, 4" straw hat, Doll hair, Raffia, Small silk sunflower and bud, Eucalyptus, Hot glue, Black permanent marker, Pinking shears, Embroidery floss

INSTRUCTIONS:

Face - Use a color copy machine to copy the photo of a face onto *Photo Effects* transfer paper (enlarge or reduce the photo to fit the doll).

Doll - Cut a slit in the back of the doll's head and remove stuffing. Using a home iron, transfer photocopy to front of head. Restuff head and whip stitch the opening closed.

Top - Use patterns to cut the dress. With right sides together, stitch bodice. Turn right side out. Trim each sleeve edge with pinking shears. Use embroidery floss to stitch around each sleeve gathering slightly. Stitch around neck opening leaving the end of thread loose. Put dress on doll. Pull thread around neckline to gather, tie off thread.

Skirt - Cut an 8" x 8" piece of fabric for skirt. With right sides together, sew side seams of skirt. Turn right side out. Trim bottom with pinking shears. Sew top of skirt with embroidery floss leaving the end of thread loose. Put the skirt on doll covering the top. Pull thread to gather, tie off.

Shoes - Use the Black permanent marker to color shoes on the doll.

Hair & Hat - Cut a 12" piece of doll hair. Fold hair in half to find the center, glue to top of head. Glue hat on head. Fold top of hat back, glue in place. Glue eucalyptus and a sunflower in the center.

Finish - Tie a raffia bow, glue it to the center of neckline. Glue a sunflower bud and leaves in the center of the raffia bow.

1 Iron photo transfer on muslin square with an iron.

2 Fuse fabric squares together and cut out flowers.

3 Glue photo border trim and backing on flowers.

Sunflower Pot

by Cyndi Hansen

MATERIALS: 3 color photos, *Hues Photo Effects* iron-on transfer paper, two 5" squares each of 3 coordinating Gold fabrics, Three 3½" squares each of muslin and Brown fabric, 2½" x 3½" piece of muslin for sign, ¼ yard of fabric for trim, Two 1" x 12" strips of torn fabric for bows, 2" x 3" piece of heavy white paper, Wood skewer, Paper-backed fusible web, Pinking shears, 5" clay pot, Dry florist foam, Sphagnum moss, Eucalyptus, Raffia, ⅞" button, Black fine-point permanent marker, Hot glue

INSTRUCTIONS:

Fabric - Use a color copy machine to copy photos onto *Photo Effects* transfer paper. Using a home iron, transfer photocopies onto muslin squares (see manufacturer's instructions). Fuse web to wrong side of muslin squares, Brown square and Gold fabric squares. Use pinking shears to cut a 2½" circle from each muslin square and a 3" circle from each Brown square. Remove paper backing.

Flowers - Remove paper backing from Gold squares and fuse to the wrong side of remaining Gold squares. Trace the sunflower patterns on white paper and cut out. Use patterns to cut sunflowers from fused Gold squares. Layer photo transfer and Brown circle in the center of sunflower. Transfer and fuse in place. Note: Cover transfers before ironing.

Pot - Glue a piece of eucalyptus to the back of each flower. Cut foam and glue in pot. Glue moss over foam. Glue fabric strip around top of pot. Tie other strip in a bow, glue bow to front of pot. Tie a raffia bow and glue it to the center of fabric bow. Glue a button in the center. Insert sunflowers in pot. Cut shorter pieces of eucalyptus and place in pot.

Sign - Fray edges of muslin piece. Fuse a 2" x 3" piece of web to wrong side of muslin. Remove paper backing and fuse to white paper. Use the Black marker to write words. Glue skewer to the back of sign and place in pot.

Sunflower Pin *by Cyndi Hansen*

MATERIALS: Color photo, *Hues Photo Effects* iron-on transfer paper, Two 4" squares of Gold fabric, 2½" square each of muslin and Brown fabric, Paper-backed fusible web, Pinking shears, Small piece of eucalyptus, Raffia, ⁹⁄₁₆" button, Pin back, Heavy white paper, Hot glue

INSTRUCTIONS:

Fabric - Use a color copy machine to copy photo onto *Photo Effects* transfer paper. Trim photo. Use an iron to transfer photo to muslin (see manufacturer's instructions). Fuse web to wrong side of muslin photo, Brown, and one Gold. Use pinking shears to cut a 2" muslin photo circle and a 2¼" Brown circle. Remove paper backing. Remove paper backing and fuse Gold to wrong side of remaining Gold square. Trace sunflower pattern on paper and cut out. Use pattern to cut sunflower from fused Gold square.

Flower - Layer photo transfer and Brownin center of sunflower. Fuse in place. Note: Cover transfer before ironing. Glue eucalyptus and pin to back of flower. Tie a raffia bow, glue to front of flower. Glue button on bow.

DOLL LEG PATTERN

DOLL BODY PATTERN

SUNFLOWER PATTERN

DOLL TOP PATTERN

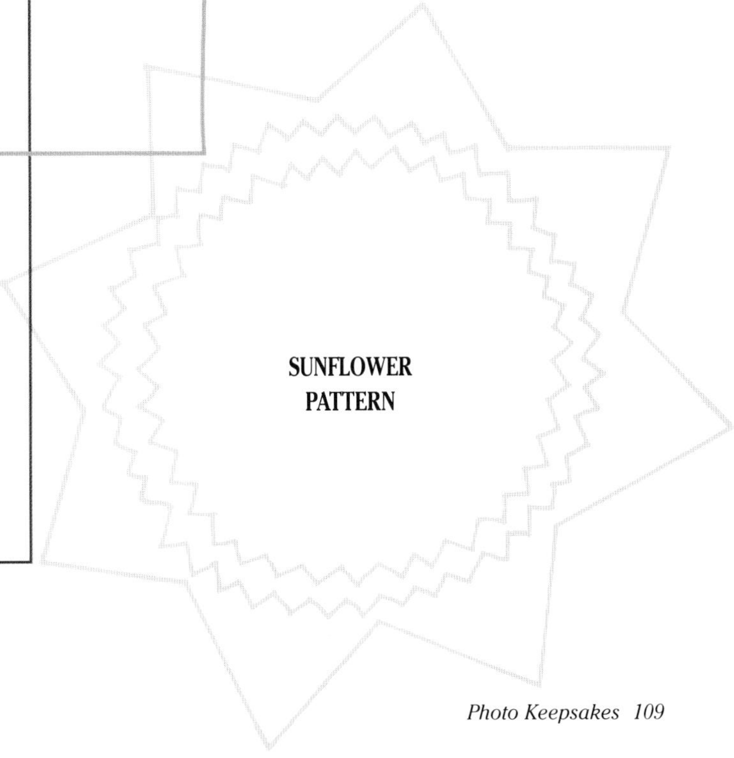

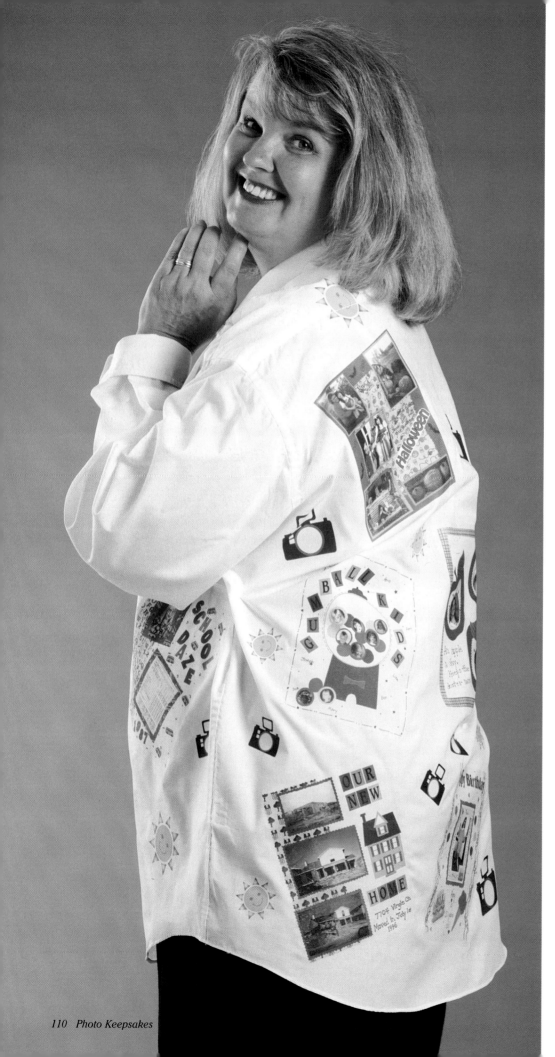

A handsome shirt covered with photographs is a wonderful attention getter. Everyone you pass will want to know who are the people decorating your shirt. So, make a wearable album from copies of your recent family Scrapbook pages.

White Goes with Everything
by Barbara Burnett

MATERIALS: Extra large white shirt, Scrapbook pages with photos, *Hues Photo Effects* iron-ontransfer paper

INSTRUCTIONS: Wash and dry shirt.

Photos - Use a color copy machine to copy Scrapbook pages, photos or images onto *Photo Effects* transfer paper (reduce pages to 8" x 10½" to fit on paper). Use a home iron to transfer copies of Scrapbook pages, photos and images on shirt (see manufacturer's instructions).

1 Reduce Scrapbook pages, make transfers with a copy machine.

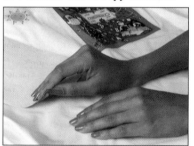

2 Arrange transfers, photos and images on shirt.

3 Fuse transfers in place with a home iron.

It's fall...bring out cool weather gear like wool blazers, jackets and vests. You'll get into the fall spirit with a great vest and follow suit with matching pants and skirts of denim.

The Blues Brothers *by Cyndi Hansen*

MATERIALS: Denim vest, 4 photos, *Hues Photo Effects* iron-on transfer paper, Muslin for transfers, Fabrics for appliques and yo-yos, Paper-backed fusible web, Assorted buttons, Pinking shears, Wash-out marking pen, Embroidery floss

INSTRUCTIONS: Wash and dry vest and applique fabrics.

Photos - Use a color copy machine to copy photos onto *Photo Effects* transfer paper. Trim photos on transfer paper. Use a home iron to transfer photos to muslin (see manufacturer's instructions). Fuse web to wrong side of muslin. Use pinking shears and pattern to trim photos into circles. Trace patterns for appliques on paper backing side of web spacing them at least 1" apart. Cut apart. Fuse patterns to applique fabrics, cut out. Remove paper backing from appliques and transfers and place on vest. Fuse in place. Note: Cover transfers before ironing.

Yo-yos - Cut two 4¼" and two 3½" circles from fabric. For each yo-yo, fold the raw edge of circle ⅛" to the wrong side. Baste close to the fold then pull thread to gather tightly. Flatten circle with gathers at the front, run needle to back and knot thread. Referring to photo, sew yo-yos in place.

Embroidery - Use a wash-out pen to mark stems and bows. Use 6 strands of Cream floss to make running stitches along the edge of vest. Use 3 strands of floss to stitch the following: Gold - running stitch sun rays, Brown - running stitch stems, Cream - lazy daisy stitch and backstitch bows, Green - lazy daisy stitch leaves, Red, Green, Gold and Cream - running stitch birdhouses, bird, and fence. Use 3 strands of floss to sew on buttons for flowers, in center of sun, bird's eye and to replace closure buttons on the vest.

See patterns on pages 116-117.

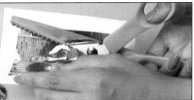

1 Trim photo transfers into circles with pinking shears.

2 Iron photos and fabric shapes onto vest with fusible web.

3 Add decorative stitching to vest with embroidery floss.

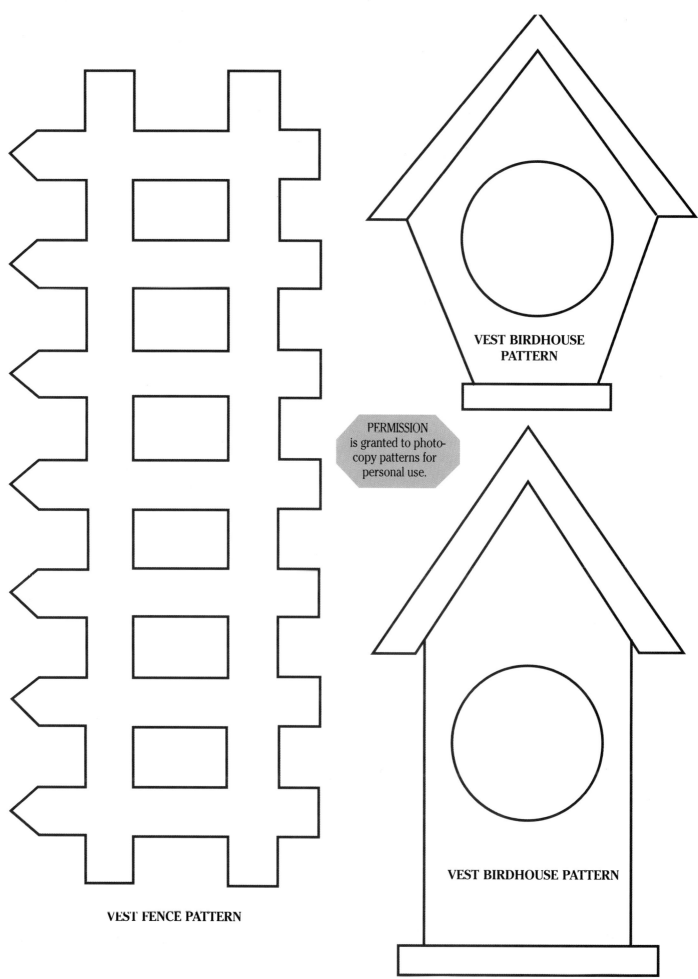

VEST BIRDHOUSE
PATTERN

PERMISSION
is granted to photo-
copy patterns for
personal use.

VEST BIRDHOUSE PATTERN

VEST FENCE PATTERN

VEST BIRD PATTERN

PERMISSION is granted to photocopy patterns for personal use.

VEST BIRDHOUSE PATTERN

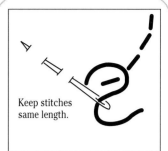

Keep stitches same length.

RUNNING STITCH

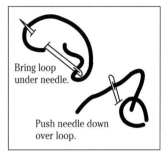

Bring loop under needle.

Push needle down over loop.

LAZY DAISY STITCH FLOWERS & LEAVES

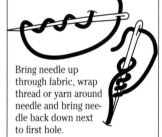

Bring needle up through fabric, wrap thread or yarn around needle and bring needle back down next to first hole.

FRENCH KNOT

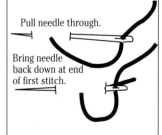

Pull needle through.

Bring needle back down at end of first stitch.

BACKSTITCH

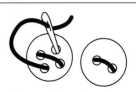

Bring needle up through one hole and down through another.

SEW ON BUTTONS

Only in America can you see a bright yellow school bus. Like the little engine that could, it chugs up and down the hills and in and around roadside stops until it picks up a load of cheery, freckled school kids.

SCHOOL BUS

Back to School   *by Cyndi Hansen*

MATERIALS: Color copy of 'School Bus' artwork, photo, *Hues Photo Effects* iron-on transfer paper, Item to decorate (3-ring notebook and *Bagworks* canvas cover for notebook, or a white T-shirt), *Wrights* Medium Red rick rack, Tiny Green rick rack, 2 small and 4 medium Red buttons for tail lights, Hot glue, Assorted colors of permanent markers

INSTRUCTIONS: 1. Make a color copy of 'School Bus'. Cut a hole in the copy.
2. Tape a photo behind artwork.
3. Copy artwork (mirror image) onto *Photo Effects* Paper.
4. Cut off excess marks. Iron onto fabric with a home iron.

Notebook Cover - Use a home iron to transfer design to canvas cover (see manufacturer's instructions).Place notebook inside of the cover. Glue buttons for tail lights and glue rick rack to the top and bottom of cover. Write names with markers.

T-shirt - Use a home iron to transfer design to T-shirt (see manufacturer's instructions).Glue buttons for tail lights and embellishments. Write names and color the sleeves with markers.

ABC - 123

1 Cross stitch design on even-weave aida cloth fabric.

2 Insert design and photo in frame.

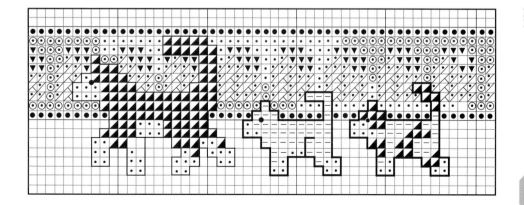

DMC Floss	Symbol	Color
806	●	Dk. Blue
822	⊙	Off White
962	✂	Lt. Pink
420	╱	Brown
Blanc	•	White
813	▼	Med. Blue
676	—	Gold
310	◣	Black

PERMISSION is granted to photocopy patterns for personal use.

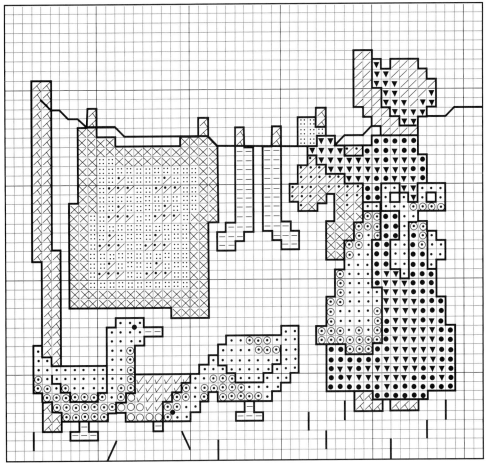

A stitch today could tell so much tomorrow. Samplers stitched many years ago are treasures today because they hold a history all their own... who made them and why? Create your own stitched treasure to pass down through the generations of your family.

A Stitch in Time

MATERIALS: Small wash board frames, 14 count Ivory aida cloth evenweave fabric, Embroidery floss, Needle, Photo
INSTRUCTIONS: Separate floss and use 2 strands for all crossstitch. Mount design and photo in frame.

PERMISSION is granted to photocopy patterns for personal use.

DMC Floss	Symbol	Color	DMC Floss	Symbol	Color
310	◢	Black	729			Golden
3687	✕	Dk. Pink	420	▲	Brown
822	⊙	Off White	996	△	Med. Blue
827	╱	Lt. Blue	910	●	Med. Green
Blanc	•	White	564	○	Lt. Green

DMC Floss	Symbol	Color
420	╱	Brown
Blanc	•	White
822	⊙	Off White
564	✓	Lt. Green
912	○	Med. Green
676	—	Gold
3687	✕	Dk. Pink
754	∷	Flesh Pink
962	╱	Lt. Pink
813	▼	Med. Blue
806	●	Dk. Blue
827	╱	Lt. Blue

Christmas Cheer

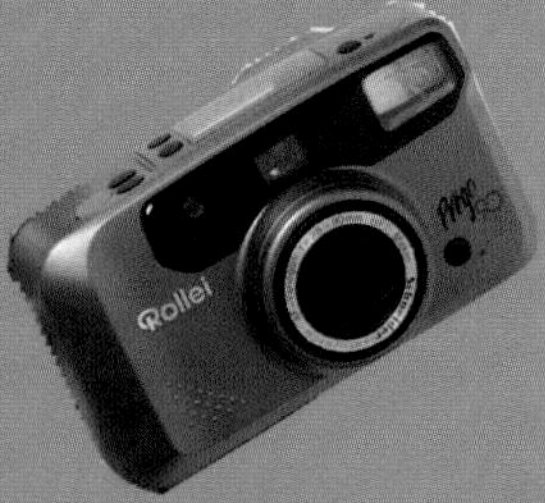
Rollei

Christmas is bringing out familiar ornaments from years of collecting. It is the fun of gathering to decorate and celebrate.

Christmas is the smell of cookies baking, the warmth thrown off by a blazing fire, the sound of voices caroling, the glow of bright lights and the closeness of family. These are the images I have captured in photographs. And now, I have also found ways to bring them out year after year.

A great many handmade Christmas decorations are ideal for embellishing with pictures. By recalling Christmases past, I keep in touch with those cherished holiday memories that have filled my life with joy.

Suzanne

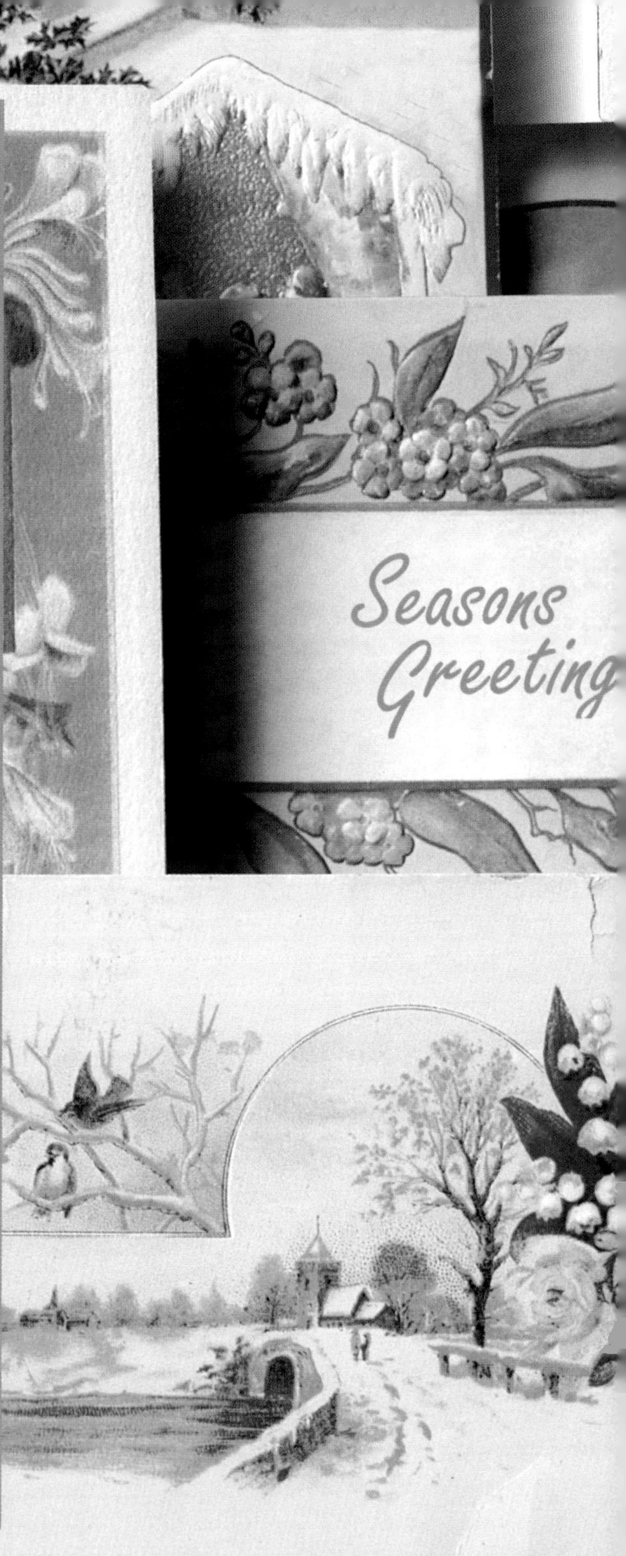
Seasons
Greeting

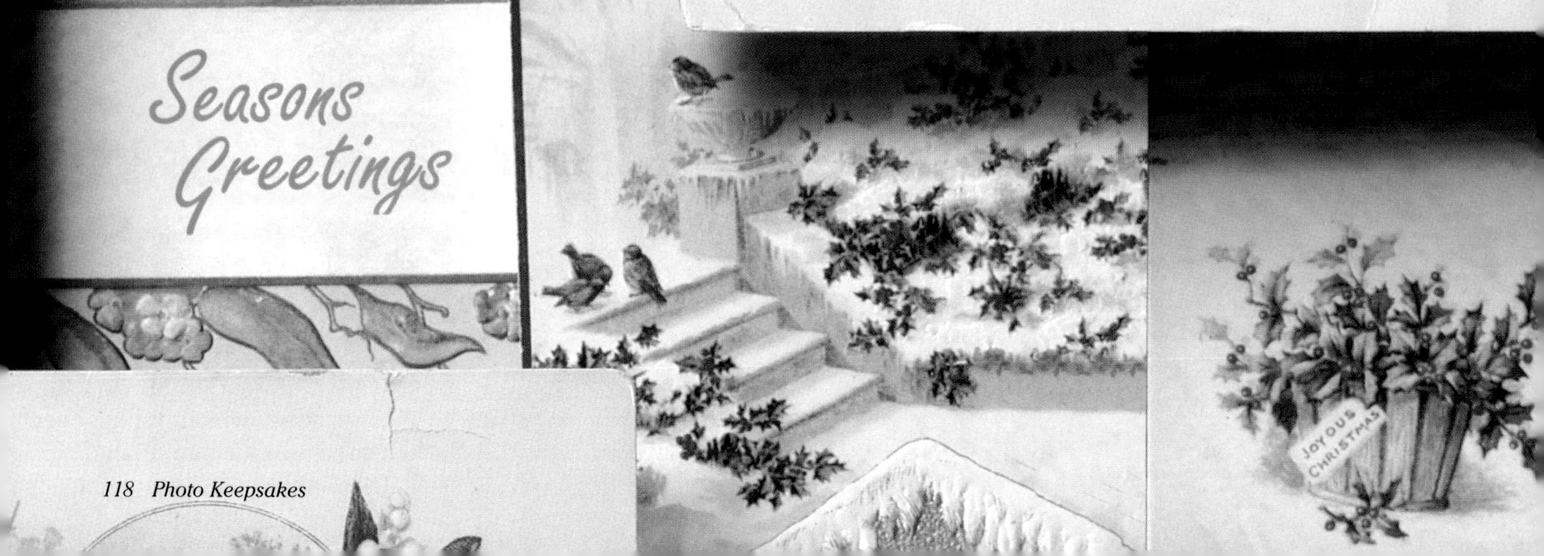
Seasons
Greetings
JOYOUS
CHRISTMAS

HOOVER-PHILA.

Christmas C

The Seasons Greetings

may your Christmas
be a happy one and the
New Year full of joy

JOYOUS
CHRISTMAS

Christmas Greetings

Seasons
Greeting

The Seasons Greetings

may your Christmas
be a happy one and the
New Year full of joy

A
Christmas
Greeting
With Best Wishes
for the New Year

1 Iron photo transfers onto muslin pieces with a home iron.

2 Fuse web to back of photos and applique fabrics.

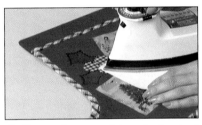

3 Cover photos and fuse to front of stocking.

4 Draw stitches on and around shapes with marker.

Be prepared for the loved ones who visit your home during the holidays. Create these heartwarming signs of the season.

All Hearts Come Home for Christmas

by Cyndi Hansen

Stocking

MATERIALS: *Bagworks* premade stocking, 2 photos, *Hues Photo Effects* iron-on transfer paper, Muslin for transfers, Fabrics for appliques and background, Five $9/16$" buttons, Paper-backed fusible web, Pinking shears, Black fine-point permanent marker, Hot glue

INSTRUCTIONS: Use a color copy machine to copy photos onto *Photo Effects* transfer paper. Trim photos on transfer paper, then use a home iron to transfer photos to muslin (see manufacturer's instructions). Fuse web to the wrong side of transfers. Use pattern to trim photos into rectangles, remove paper backing. Trace patterns for backgrounds and appliques onto the paper side of web spacing them at least 1" apart. Cut appliques apart. Fuse web to the wrong side of background fabric and applique fabrics. Cut out rectangles and use pinking shears to cut out holly and berries. Remove paper backing. Arrange all appliques on the front of stocking

See additional patterns on page 122.

using photo as a guide. Fuse in place. Note: Cover photo transfers with muslin. Use a marker to draw stitching lines on holly. Glue buttons in the centers of berries.

Tree Skirt

MATERIALS: *Bagworks* premade tree skirt, 10 photos, *Hues Photo Effects* iron-on transfer paper, Muslin for transfers, Fabrics for appliques and background, 20" square of fabric for tree, Fifteen $5/8$" Red buttons, Six $5/8$" Cream buttons, Paper-backed fusible web, Pinking shears, Black fine-point permanent marker, Hot glue, Twine

INSTRUCTIONS: Use a color copy machine to copy photos onto *Photo Effects* transfer paper. Trim photos on transfer paper, then use a home iron to transfer photos to muslin (see manufacturer's instructions). Use pinking shears and pattern to trim photos into circles. Trace patterns for backgrounds, appliques, and tree onto paper side of web spacing them at least 1" apart, cut apart. Fuse web to wrong side of fabrics. Remove paper backing. Arrange all appliques on front of tree skirt. Fuse in place. Note: Cover photo transfers with muslin. Use marker to write letters and draw stitching lines on holly and packages. For bows on packages, loop twine back and forth to form 4 to 6 loops. Tie off bow with a small length of twine. Make 9 hand-made bows for tree. Glue twine for garland and bows as shown.

PERMISSION is granted to photo-copy patterns for personal use.

TREE SKIRT GIFT PATTERN

TREE SKIRT GIFT PATTERN

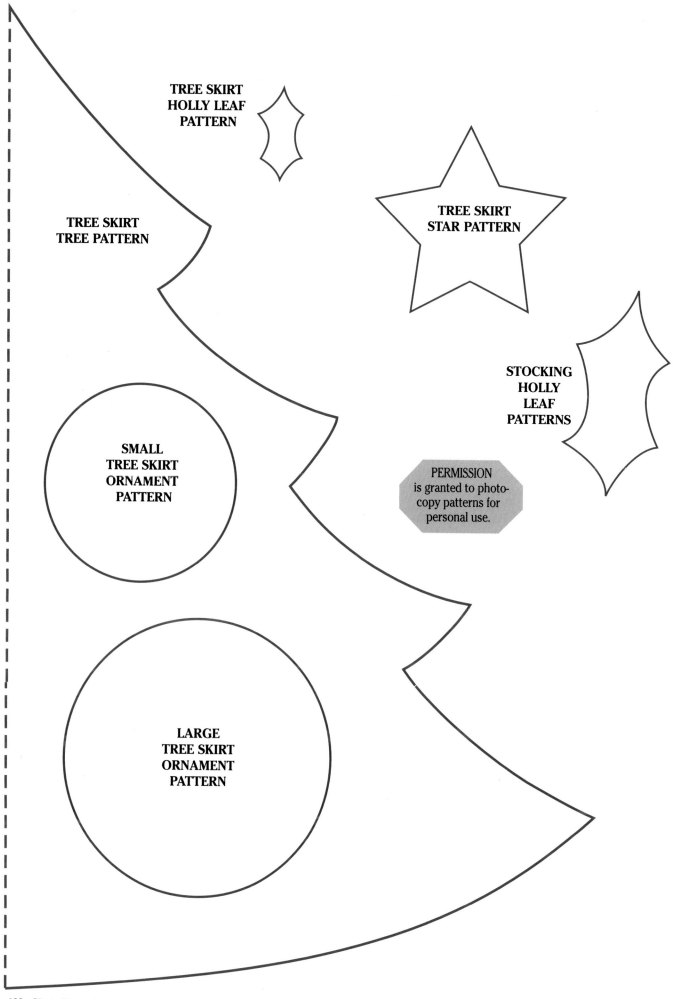

TREE SKIRT
HOLLY LEAF
PATTERN

TREE SKIRT
STAR PATTERN

TREE SKIRT
TREE PATTERN

STOCKING
HOLLY
LEAF
PATTERNS

SMALL
TREE SKIRT
ORNAMENT
PATTERN

PERMISSION
is granted to photo-
copy patterns for
personal use.

LARGE
TREE SKIRT
ORNAMENT
PATTERN

Half the fun of the holidays is in the decorating and preparations that go into getting ready for an exciting occasion. Help your little ones really experience the joys of the season with decorated plates.

Milk & Cookies

Glass Plate *by Cyndi Hansen*

MATERIALS: Photo, Clear glass plate, *Delta Perm Enamels*, *Plaid Royal Coat* Decoupage Finish, Sponge brush, Paint brushes, Wavy edge scissors

INSTRUCTIONS: Clean plate with vinegar and water. Use a color copy machine to enlarge the phto on white cardstock paper. Trim photocopy to fit in center of plate. Apply a thin coat of decoupage finish/glue to front of photocopy, press to back of plate. Rub fingers across copy to press out any air bubbles, let dry. Apply another light coat of decoupage finish/glue to back of copy, let dry. Turn plate over and place it on top of the pattern. Using a brush, paint designs, allowing to dry between colors. Turn plate over and paint back of plate white, let dry. Use a flat brush to apply *Perm Enamel* Clear gloss glaze over the entire plate.

Wall Hanging

MATERIALS: 3 photos, *Hues Photo Effects* iron-on transfer paper, three 4 x 4½" pieces of muslin for photos, 15¼" x 2¼" piece of muslin for wording, 21 x 12" piece of fabric for pocket, Two 22 x 11¾" pieces of fabric for front and back of wall hanging, 22 x 11¾" piece of quilt batting, Fabric for tabs and yo-yos, Paper-backed fusible web, 4 Red and 4 Yellow ¾" buttons, 3 Red and 2 Yellow 1" buttons, 2 White ⅜" buttons for yo-yos, Embroidery floss, Pinking shears, Black fine-point permanent marker

INSTRUCTIONS: **Photos** - Use a color copy machine to copy photos onto *Photo Effects* transfer paper. Trim photos on transfer paper, then use a home iiron to transfer photos to fabric (see manufacturer's instructions). Fuse web to wrong side of transfers. Trim pieces with pinking shears, remove paper backing. Arrange muslin pieces. Fuse transfers in place. Note: Cover transfer with muslin before ironing. Layer wall hanging back, batting, front and pocket, pin together.

Wording - Fray edges of muslin. Use marker to write words. Cut a piece of web slightly smaller than muslin and fuse to the wrong side. Remove paper backing and fuse wording to wall hanging.

Yo-yos - Cut two 3½" circles from fabric. For each yo-yo, fold raw edge of circle ⅛" to wrong side. Baste close to fold, pull thread to gather tightly. Flatten circle with gathers at the front, run needle to back and knot thread. Sew on yo-yos with a button in center of each.

Finish - Use embroidery floss and running stitch to sew around wall hanging, along sides and bottom of pocket, along top edge of pocket (do not stitch closed) and between transfers to form separate pockets. Cut five 2" x 5" strips for hang tabs. For each tab, fold wrong sides of each long edge to center and press. Fold each tab in half and pin to back of wall hanging. Sew tabs in place with a button on the front. Sew a button to corner of each pocket.

1 Glue trimmed photo to plate. Apply a second coat of glue.

2 Place plate over pattern and paint designs. Add dots with a brush handle.

3 Paint the back of plate white. Apply *Perm Enamel* glaze over the entire plate.

See Patterns on page 133

Terra cotta bells bring year round cheer. Create music with jingling beauties showcasing your favorite photos and faces.

Jingle Bells, Photo Bells

by Delores Frantz

MATERIALS: Three 3" clay pots, 3 small photos, 54" of White/Gold 3mm cord, Matte finish clear acrylic spray, Red, Green, Yellow, White and Metallic Gold acrylic paint, Black permanent marker, 3 Gold 25mm jingle bells, Wavy edge scissors, Goop glue

INSTRUCTIONS: Spray pots with clear acrylic.

Paint - Pots White, Red and Green. Transfer patterns to rim of pots and paint designs. White pot - Red berries and Green holly with Gold outline. Red pot - Gold stars. Green pot - Red and Yellow bulbs, Gold bulb bases and Black marker cord.

Photos - Use wavy scissors to cut 1½" circles from photos (or color copies of photos). Glue to side of pot. Paint Gold dots around photos. Use a marker to write name and date on the back of each pot.

Hanger - Cut cord into three 18" pieces. Thread bell on cord and position 4" from cord end. Fold 4" up and place it against remaining cord. Hold cord end and remaining cord together. Tie an overhand knot. Thread long cord through pot and out hole. Place knot against hole. Thread cord back down through hole leaving an 8" loop on top. Tie an overhand knot against top of bell. Trim ends of cord.

1 Spray pots with clear acrylic. Paint entire pot one color.

2 Paint design on rim of pot. Outline leaves with Gold.

3 Trim photos into circles with wavy scissors and glue to pot.

4 Thread a long cord through the pot and out the hole. Tie a knot.

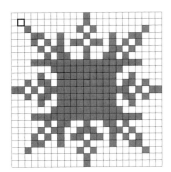

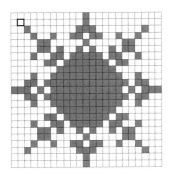

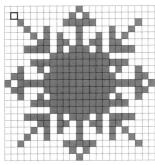

Gazing up at the starlit sky provides the perfect opportunity to make a wish…It may even come true for the holidays. These wonderful photo snowflakes make the stars twinkle indoors, too. You can never make too many wishes!

Twinkle, Twinkle Little Snowflake

by Delores Frantz

MATERIALS: White 7 count plastic canvas, *Duncan - Tulip* White Pearl dimensional paint, 27" of Gold lamé thread, Heavy cardboard, Plastic bag, Wavy edge scissors, 3 small photos, GOOP glue

INSTRUCTIONS:

Snowflakes - Following pattern, cut snowflake shapes from plastic canvas using small scissors or a craft knife. Place shapes face up on cardboard covered with plastic. Hold the paint bottle straight up and down with the tip slightly inside the square to be painted. Gently squeeze the bottle and fill each square very full. The paint will bleed out the bottom of the square and seal the back of the canvas. Do not move shapes or paint will smear. Let snowflakes dry on the plastic covered cardboard for 12 hours. Gently peel snowflakes off plastic, turn over and let dry 12 more hours.

Hanger - Thread 9" of Gold thread through hanger square. Hold thread ends together and tie an overhand knot. Use wavy scissors to cut photo into 1½" circle. Glue photo to snowflake. Note: Since the paint has a tendency to stick to itself, store each snowflake separately in a plastic bag.

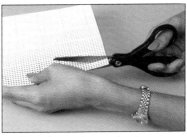

1 Cut shape from plastic canvas with scissors or craft knife.

2 Fill holes in canvas with dimensional paint.

*P*ilgrims used wool felt to make blankets warm and protect against the cold of winter. In folk art designs, busy hands incorporated basic shapes to use felt for applique and symbolic motifs. Holidays remind us of days past. These ornaments showcase those memories and make a heartwarming gift for your family.

Warm Memories

by Cyndi Hansen

MATERIALS: Photos, *Hues Photo Effects* iron-on transfer paper, Cream, Red, Green, Blue and Gold felt, Quilt batting, Embroidery floss, Assorted buttons, Heavy-duty paper-backed fusible web, White paper, Pinking shears

INSTRUCTIONS:

Photos - Use a color copy machine to copy photos onto *Photo Effects* transfer paper. Trim photos on transfer paper into circles, then use a home iron to transfer photos to Cream felt, (see manufacturer's instructions). Fuse web to wrong side of transfer. Trace patterns onto white paper and cut out. Use patterns and pinking shears to cut out shapes from colored felt.

Stocking - Cut out stocking pieces, hanger and batting. Layer stocking pieces and pin in place. Fuse photo transfer to center of stocking. Note: Cover transfer with muslin before ironing. Use running stitch and embroidery floss to sew around stocking and to sew on buttons.

Tree - Cut out tree, batting and stars. Layer tree pieces and batting, pin in place. Fuse photo transfer to center of tree. Note: Cover transfer with muslin before ironing. Pin stars to front and back of tree. Use running stitch and embroidery floss to sew around star and to sew garland on tree. Sew on buttons.

Mitten - Cut out mitten, mitten top, hanger and batting. Layer mitten pieces and batting, pin in place. Fuse photo transfer to center of mitten. Note: Cover transfer with muslin before ironing. Use embroidery floss and running stitch to stitch around mitten and top piece. Add buttons.

Hanger - Add a floss hanger to each felt ornament.

1 Trim each photo transfer into a circle. Transfer onto a piece of Cream felt with a home iron.

3 Cover and fuse a Cream felt circle to the center front of large felt shape.

2 Trace patterns onto white paper, cut out. Use patterns and pinking shears to cut out shapes.

4 Layer batting and felt shapes then sew layers together with a running stitch. Sew on buttons.

WARM MEMORIES PATTERNS

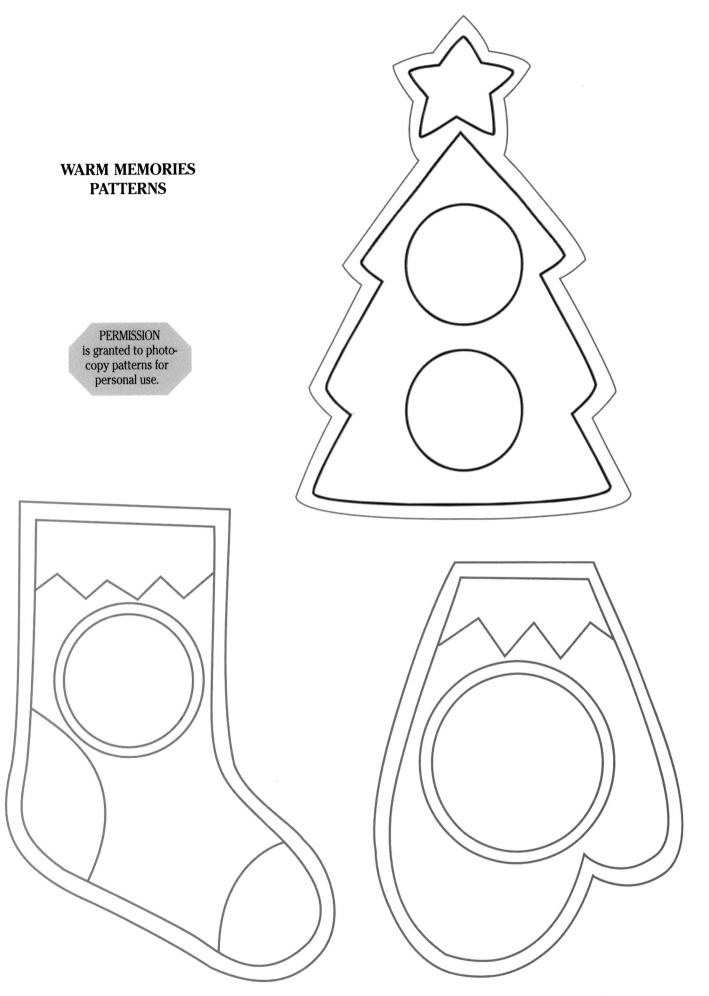

A Family Tree & Birdhouse Mats

by Cyndi Hansen

MATERIALS FOR EACH MAT: Frame (8 x 10" for small tree, 11 x 14" for large family tree), Photos, Bristol board or cardstock paper, Colored pencils, White eraser, Clear acrylic sealer, Black fine-point permanent marker, Craft knife

INSTRUCTIONS: Trace and transfer pattern to Bristol board or cardstock paper. Draw outlines with Black marker. Cut out holes with a sharp Craft knife. Color design with colored pencils working from top to bottom or left to right so as not to smudge design. Blow off excess color as needed and rub off mistakes with White eraser. Seal design with 2 light coats of sealer, allow to dry between coats. Tape photos to back of mat and secure in frame.

See patterns on pages 130-132.

1 Draw design with a Black marker. Color tree with colored pencils.

2 Tape photos to back of mat and secure in frame.

PERMISSION
is granted to photo-
copy patterns for
personal use.

11" x 14" FRAME

PERMISSION
is granted to photo-
copy patterns for
personal use.

FACES FRAME
PATTERNS
Page 62

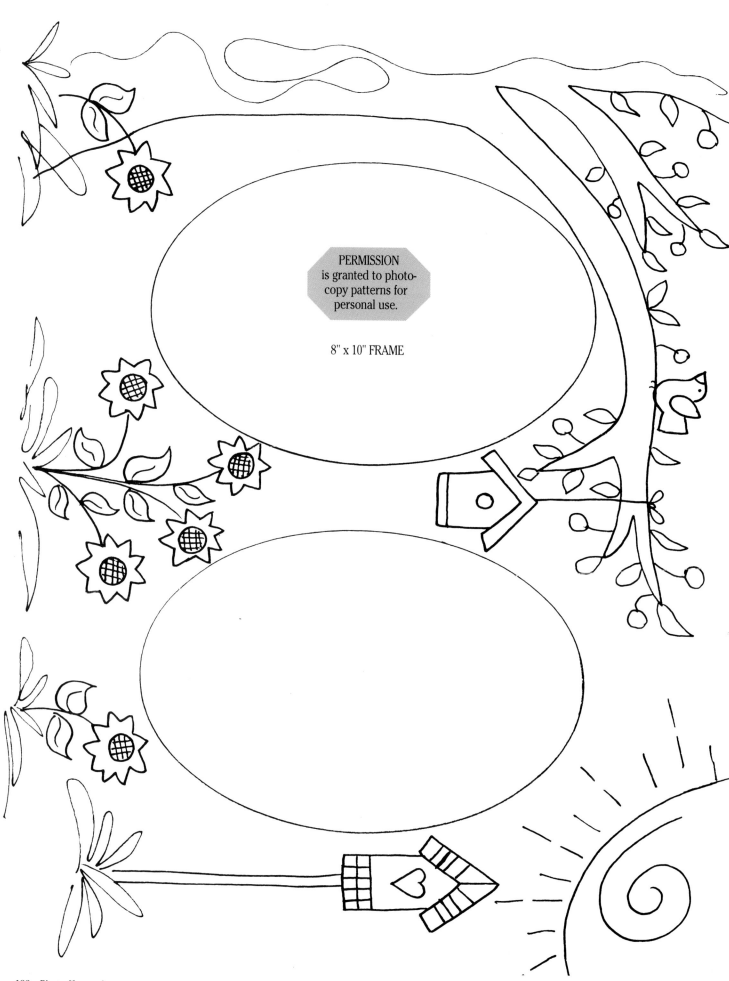

PERMISSION
is granted to photo-
copy patterns for
personal use.

8" x 10" FRAME

MILK & COOKIES PLATE PATTERN

PERMISSION is granted to photo-copy patterns for personal use.

WALL HANGING PATTERN

Greet visitors to your yard with stepping stones made by your family and friends. Create a special stone for birthdays, holidays, special days, vacation memories or just for special occasions.

Each stone will represent a milestone in your family life and adventures. Add shells collected at the seashore, pebbles from the creek, stones from the mountains. Collections from everywhere will soon grace your yard and home with mementoes from special places and memories of special times.

Life tumbles along presenting obstacles. Making a memory stone with the helping hands of children is the perfect way to christen a new stone path.

Stepping Stones

by Milestones

MATERIALS: *Milestones* StoneCraft round stepping stone kit, Colored glass stones, Small heart tiles, Heart shape cookie cutter

INSTRUCTIONS: Following kit instructions, add color if desired and stir water into stone mix. Pour mix into mold and use a mixing paddle to smooth the surface. Plan your design. Use a cookie cutter to make heart designs and a craft stick to write words. Push stones and tiles in place. Allow stone to dry. Remove from the form.

1 Add water to stone mix following the manufacturer's instructions.

2 Pour mixture into stepping stone form.

3 Press designs (cookie cutters, etc.) into wet mixture.

4 Push stones and tiles in mixture to complete the design.

Have you ever seen the light in a little one's eyes when his picture and report card are prominently displayed on the refrigerator door? The bragging begins and it is truly a moment of fame. Showcase your family's special moments on a brag board made to hang attractively in any room.

Photo Holder
Memory Brag Board
by Virginia Reynolds

MATERIALS: 18" square of *Hunt* foamcore board, 18" square piece of quilt batting, ⅔ yard (24" square) of Burgundy fabric, 25 thumbtacks, 13 Burgundy 1" buttons, 9 yards of ⅜" heart print ribbon, Hot glue

INSTRUCTIONS:

Batting - Glue batting to front of foamcore board. Hot glue in spots to secure to the board.

Fabric - Place fabric over batting. Turn project over. Fold and stretch edges of fabric over the edges of foamcore board then hot glue (or staple) securely in place. If needed trim corners for a smooth fit.

Ribbon - Cut ribbon into two 26", four 18" and four 9" pieces. Place two long pieces in an **X** on the front side and wrap the ends around the board. Secure corners and center of ribbon with thumbtacks. Space 18" length pieces 4¼" from the **X**. Place 9" pieces 4¼" from medium pieces and adjust so ribbons meet properly. Secure in place with thumbtacks at ends and intersections.

Buttons - Glue buttons over tacks. If desired, make a hanger from left over ribbon.

1 Glue batting to front of board, fold over and glue edges to back.

2 Place fabric over batting, fold ends of fabric over edges of board and glue into place.

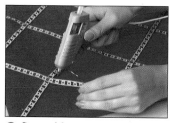

3 Cut ribbon to length and arrange. Tack in place. Secure ends / intersections with glue.

4 Glue a button over ribbon at each intersection. Insert photos under ribbons.

Cheerful Christmas fabrics combined with cherished cards...what a wonderful way to celebrate the season. Share your messages with all who celebrate in your home by displaying them in a beautiful Christmas Card Holder. You will make memories for years to come.

Christmas Card Holder

by Pam Hammons

MATERIALS: 16" x 20" piece of *Hunt* foamcore board, ⅔ yard each of 5 Red/Green/Off White solid and print fabrics, Hot glue

INSTRUCTIONS: From each piece of fabric cut two 12" x 24" strips. Glue the bottom edge of a strip 9" down from the top of foamcore board. Fold and glue 2" of fabric to the back of foamcore board at the top and sides. Fold remaining fabric strips in half lengthwise. Referring to photo, glue the bottom edges of each strip to board or to the underlying fabric. Fold and stretch the edges of fabric to the back and hot glue in place. The bottom pocket is 4" high with 2" of each edge glued to the back.

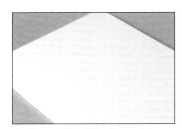

1 Cut a 16" x 20" piece of foamcore board for the backing.

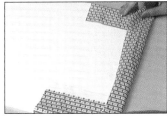

2 Fold 2" of fabric to back at top and sides, glue in place.

3 Glue bottom edges of folded strips to front and sides to back.

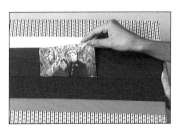

4 Insert Christmas cards and photos into pockets.

A room with everything in its place offers comfort and a sense of belonging. Any paper, photograph, keepsake or tool is easy to find. If you need more storage but want it to be attractive, add some special details to an ordinary box.

Acid-Free Storage Boxes

by Audrey Kammer

MATERIALS: *Corruboard®* Acid-Free Basics storage boxes, 1 yard of House Panel print and ½ yard of button print fabric for each box, Buttons, 4 wood hearts, Green acrylic paint, sponge brush, two 18" lengths of ribbon, Black permanent marker, Hot glue, *ThermO Web Peel n Stick* double sided adhesive

INSTRUCTIONS: Assemble boxes (see manufacturer's instructions). Referring to photo, cut and adhere pieces of fabric to boxes. Paint wood hearts and glue on box. Make 'stitches' around drawers and panels with Black marker. Make a latch with 2 large buttons and ribbon. Glue remaining buttons as design accents.

1 Assemble box carefully following the manufacturer's instructions.

2 Cut fabric pieces to decorate box referring to photo for placement.

3 Adhere fabric to box with hot glue or with double sided adhesive sheets.

4 Glue buttons together for latch. Tie closed with a ribbon loop.

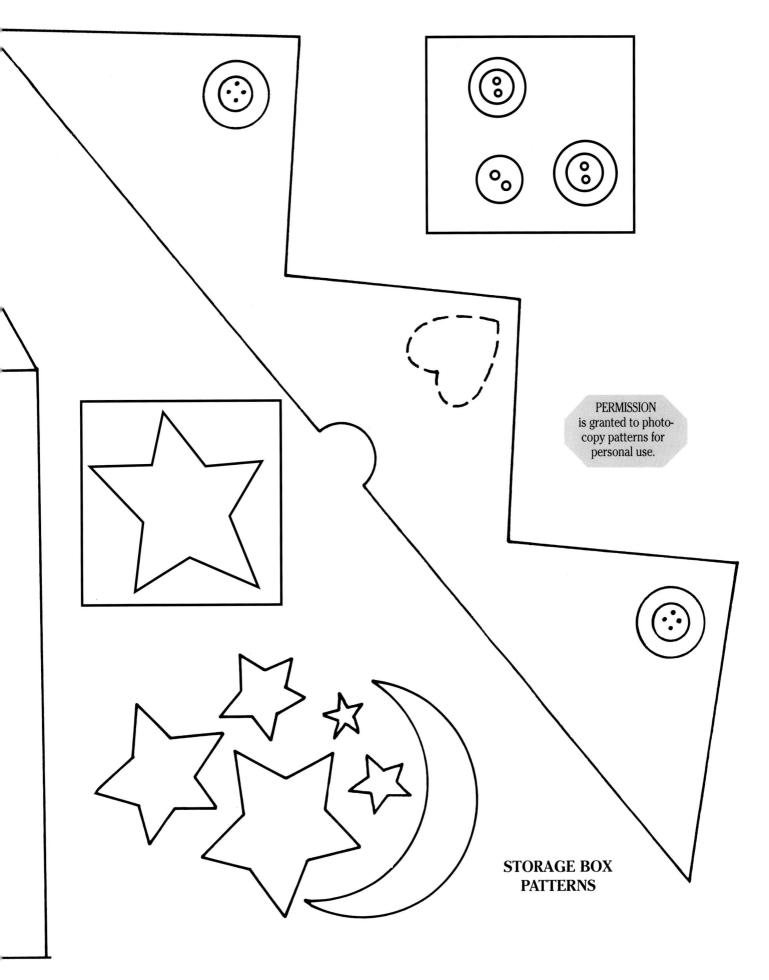

PERMISSION
is granted to photo-
copy patterns for
personal use.

**STORAGE BOX
PATTERNS**

In vintage boxes I found pictures of my mother, Nanny, and sisters. For many years we organized an annual "girls only" trip to Guatemala or Mexico. We took rolls of photographs, collected artisan crafts like "huipiles" and hand carved and painted "animales", and spent days discovering the culture and countryside. What I find in these photos brings back so many memories.

The trips to Latin America where we all bond as mother and sisters still continue once a year even though each has moved on to another stage in life. My sister Amy, an artist, has moved to Santa Fe. Brendy has small children and lives five hours away, and my mom still works everyday in her yard and garden.

Although the days of traveling together are fewer, the keepsakes, photos and memories are constant reminders of those wonderful heartfelt experiences.

Suzanne

Index of Photo Keepsakes Source of Supplies

The Perfect Ending

When my friends and family get together the best memories are made. It's a time when people come from far and near to share with one another. And when they all depart we feel sadness but are then reminded of the wealth of everlasting memories.

So many wonderful people made this book possible. A sincere "Thank You" to all the designers who created such wonderful Photo Keepsake projects.

And "Thanks" to all my family and friends for sharing their own keepsakes, treasures, and remembrances to make this book full of cherished mementos.

Suzanne